Magic Quizdom

Disneylandia Minutiae Semper Absurda

Kevin Yee and Jason Schultz

Second Edition

Zauberreich Press
Orlando, Florida

Magic Quizdom: Disneylandia Minutiae Semper Absurda
by Kevin Yee and Jason Schultz

Published by
ZAUBERREICH PRESS
Orlando, Florida
http://www.zauberreichpress.com

Cover design by "The Dozak"

This book makes reference to various Disney copyrighted characters,
trademarks, marks, and registered marks owned by The Walt Disney
Company and Disney Enterprises, Inc.

Magic Quizdom is not endorsed by, sponsored by, or connected with
The Walt Disney Company and/or Disney Enterprises, Inc. in any
way.

Library of Congress Control Number: 2003102305
ISBN: 0-9728398-0-1

SECOND EDITION
Printed in the United States of America

To our mothers.

We are indebted to many people for help with research, including **Bruce Gordon, Eddie Sotto, Bob Gurr, Chris Merritt, Josh Shipley, Russell Brower, Bill Watkins,** and many others too numerous to mention. **Scott L Jordan** provided general advice and suggested the title of the book.

A special acknowledgement must go to **David Smith** for bringing his unique and apparently limitless stores of Disney knowledge to bear while proofreading and copyediting. **Margaret Adamic**, the staff at Disney Publishing, and the staff at the Walt Disney Archives shepherded us with grace and patience through much of revision process, and ensured that we overstepped no legal boundaries.

Thanks also go to our friends and proofreaders **Jacob Kahla, Todd Parker,** and **Marty Klein,** the latter especially for his consistent attempts to hammer good writing habits into us.

Lastly, the greatest thanks must go to the man who started it all, **Walt Disney**. It is his dream we inhabit, and we are all the better for it.

Foreword

As eternal fans of the original Disneyland, we've been surrounded since birth with the rich history and trivia that abounds in Walt's magical Park. This book is designed to serve as a complement to the existing books out there that offer general Disney trivia. We wanted to create a book that examined and explained the trivia of Disneyland in particular. The past decades have been kind to Disneyland, and its history continues to enthrall us even as it marches inexorably forward. We hope you'll notice two subtle themes creeping into our questions. First, that Disneyland is often the leader in introducing new concepts to the theme park industry with innovations in themed concepts, ride systems, and designs; and second, that Disneyland often pays tributes to its earlier history, other resorts, and previous ideas, weaving them together in a kind of theme park synergy.

We all associate Disneyland with the good times we had when we were younger. Rides, characters, and set pieces get recycled, history overlaps with the present and the future, and the nostalgic symbols of the past both remind us of the good times gone by and encourage us to make new happy memories. It's these little touches that bestow such magic on Walt's Disneyland and keep it special, though some of them may be so subtle that many visitors miss the connections. This book is our effort to shine a light on those connections, render them visible to all, and thus make the magic they create that much more apparent. For us, knowing the details doesn't spoil the magic — it clarifies, amplifies, and in a way helps to create it. After all, this is Walt Disney's "Magic" Kingdom. Disneyland is like a laboratory, constantly experimenting and innovating. Knowing Disneyland's history enables us to see it as a living and evolving entity on a journey, one which is exciting, relevant, and fresh to us today, and it keeps us looking forward to the future.

— Kevin and Jason

Main Street, U.S.A.

Main Street, U.S.A.
Questions

Section One - Easy

1. Main Street, U.S.A. is based on Walt's hometown. What is that often-mentioned town?
    a. Marceline, Missouri
    b. Manchester, Missouri
    c. Marionville, Missouri
    d. Marquand, Missouri

2. What is significant about many of the Main Street Windows?
    a. They are all shaded pink
    b. There were all made using Venetian glass
    c. They have the names of important contributors to Disneyland on them
    d. They were personally installed by Walt Disney

3. Where on Main Street can you listen to party-line telephones?
    a. Disney Showcase

b. Market House

c. Emporium

d. New Century Timepieces

4. Where is Walt Disney's private apartment located?

    a. Behind the Opera House

    b. Behind City Hall

    c. Above the Fire Station

    d. Above the Opera House

5. Which is the largest shop at Disneyland?

    a. Disneyana

    b. Disney Showcase

    c. Disney Clothiers

    d. Emporium

6. Which is not one of the vehicles that has traveled on Main Street through the years?

    a. Horse-drawn fire wagon

    b. Horse-drawn surrey

    c. Electric parade surrey

    d. Electric trolley

7. How is there a little slice of the Burbank Disney Studios on Main Street?

    a. Elm trees from Burbank were transplanted to Main Street

    b. A slice of Walt's pepperoni pizza was implanted in the City Hall plaster walls

c. Walt's offices were transplanted to the Opera House

d. Parts of the Ink & Paint building were used as the cornerstone for the Main Street Train Station

8. What was added to the Disneyland Railroad in 1966?
    a. A third steam engine
    b. Passenger cars, replacing cattle cars
    c. Grand Canyon Diorama
    d. Primeval World Diorama

9. Where is the Hotel Marceline?
    a. Above the Market House
    b. Above Carnation Café
    c. Next to the Gibson Girl
    d. Next to the Silhouette Studio

10. What two "arcades" are located on Main Street?
    a. Crystal Arcade and Main Street Arcade
    b. Penny Arcade and Starcade
    c. Penny Arcade and Crystal Arcade
    d. Penny Arcade and Main Street Arcade

11. Which movie has never run in the Main Street Cinema?
    a. *Mickey's Polo Team*
    b. *The Old Mill*
    c. *The Dognapper*
    d. *Traffic Trouble*

12. How have some cars of the Disneyland Railroad changed since Disneyland first opened?
    a. Remodeled to passenger cars
    b. Extended by ten feet
    c. Wide gauge chassis replaced by narrow gauge
    d. Speakers replaced by Dolby Digital Audio system

13. Throughout the years, which film company has never sponsored a shop on Main Street?
    a. Kodak
    b. GAF
    c. Polaroid
    d. Fuji

14. What did the Carnation Ice Cream Parlor become in 1997?
    a. Carnation Plaza Gardens
    b. Carnation Terrace
    c. Carnation Café
    d. Main Street Café

15. Approximately how long is the Disneyland Railroad track?
    a. 0.5 miles
    b. 1.5 miles
    c. 2.5 miles
    d. 3.5 miles
    e. 4.5 miles
    f. 5.5 miles

16. What is the name of the statue in the middle of the Central Plaza?
    a. Friends
    b. Companions
    c. Soulmates
    d. Partners
    e. Walt
    f. Mickey

17. Who is the Honorary Mayor of Disneyland, according to a window above City Hall?
    a. Mickey Mouse
    b. Walt Disney
    c. Roy Disney
    d. Michael Eisner
    e. Paul Pressler
    f. Jack Lindquist

18. What is the significance of the electric car formerly on display in the Walt Disney Story exhibit at the Opera House?
   a. Walt's personal car for the Studios
   b. Walt's guest parade car
   c. Roy's personal car
   d. It was built from the wreckage of a horse-drawn trolley
   e. Walt built it himself
   f. Roy built it himself

19. What was the original finale music for Great Moments with Mr. Lincoln?
   a. "Golden Dream"
   b. "Star-Spangled Banner"
   c. "God Bless America"
   d. "National Emblem March"
   e. "Battle Hymn of the Republic"
   f. "Stars and Stripes Forever"

20. The owl formerly in the Walt Disney Story, at the Opera House, originated from what Disney movie?
   a. *The Reluctant Dragon*
   b. *Make Mine Music*
   c. *Fun and Fancy Free*
   d. *Melody Time*
   e. *Song of the South*
   f. *So Dear to My Heart*

21. What scale is the Disneyland Railroad?
    a. Full-size
    b. Three-fourths
    c. Five-eighths
    d. One-half
    e. One-quarter
    f. One-eighth

22. What kind of music plays on Main Street?
    a. Showtunes and jazz
    b. Country and western
    c. Ragtime and showtunes
    d. Swing and jazz
    e. Mambo and new age
    f. Salsa and swing

23. Who designed the Main Street vehicles?
    a. Marc Davis
    b. Bob Gurr
    c. Herb Ryman
    d. Tommy Walker
    e. Bill Evans
    f. Buzz Price

24. What was the Opera House used for before the Babes in Toyland Exhibit moved in?
    a. Great Moments with Mr. Lincoln
    b. Security station
    c. Fire department
    d. Lumber mill

e. Sign shop

f. Metal shop

25. Who sang "Two Brothers" in Great Moments with Mr. Lincoln?
    a. Alicia Almo
    b. Pat Boone
    c. Edith Piaf
    d. Diana Ross
    e. Tina Turner
    f. Grace Kelley

26. What is the elevation of Disneyland, as given on the Main Street Train Station?
    a. 124 feet above sea level
    b. 128 feet above sea level
    c. 134 feet above sea level
    d. 138 feet above sea level
    e. 144 feet above sea level
    f. 148 feet above sea level

27. For whom is Disneyland's fifth train engine named?
    a. Walt Disney
    b. Roy Disney
    c. Ward Kimball
    d. Roger Broggie
    e. Harper Goff
    f. Bob Gurr

Section Three - Difficult

28. What was the original name of the Plaza Inn?

29. What planned area next to the Market House gave rise to the idea of a talking Confucius head?

30. Town Square Café had three other names during periods when it was hosted by outside companies. What were they?

31. What names has the Kennel had?

32. Which speeches of Abraham Lincoln's did we hear in Great Moments with Mr. Lincoln prior to 2001?

33. Who became the voice of Abraham Lincoln when the attraction was altered to show a single speech at Gettysburg?

34. Which sponsors on Main Street have been there since Park opening?

35. How is "forced perspective" utilized on Main Street?

36. What did the Kalamazoo Manufacturing Company give to Walt, who promptly installed it in Disneyland?

37. Who painted the slides for the original Great Moments with Mr. Lincoln presentation?

38. What are the origins of the model of the U.S. Capitol building in Great Moments with Mr. Lincoln?

Main Street, U.S.A.
Answers

Section One - Easy

1. <u>Main Street, U.S.A. is based on Walt's hometown. What is that often-mentioned town?</u> A. Marceline, Missouri. He actually only lived in Marceline for a few years, but they deeply impressed him in a way that his other childhood cities did not, such as Chicago (he was too young) or Kansas City (where he was put to work delivering newspapers). It was also in Marceline that he began his lifelong obsession with trains; there he would often run out to view the passing trains each morning. His first job would later be as a news butcher, selling candy and newspapers on trains. He also spent time in Kissimmee, Florida — very near the future home of Walt Disney World — during his youth. Though Marceline is the primary inspiration, it's not the only one. Designers also drew from memories of Fort Collins, Colorado, and Goderich, Ontario. Nor is Main Street an actual depiction of life in small towns in 1900, but rather an idealized version. It's also universalized by calling it Main Street, U.S.A. — this is a representation of ANY American town at the turn of the twentieth century.

2. <u>What is significant about many of the Main Street Windows?</u> C. They honor individuals who have had a significant impact on Disneyland's development and history. One of the original men honored was Walt's father, Elias Disney, who is given the profession of "Contractor" — also his real life occupation. His window is located above the Emporium.

3. <u>Where on Main Street can you listen to party-line telephones?</u>
B. The Market House. These recordings, set in the 1890s, are another touch of theming that sets the Disney Parks one step ahead of the competition. From 1998-2002, the Disneyland Forever kiosks in Tomorrowland and Main Street sold this recording, along with many other familiar Disneyland sounds, using a "music-on-demand" technology pioneered by Digital-on-Demand (in a subsidiary called RedDotNet).

4. <u>Where is Walt Disney's private apartment located?</u> C. Above the Fire Station. This location in Town Square was especially useful during the Park's construction — it was a long drive back to his Holmby Hills home and Walt was usually there until late at night and arrived early in the morning.

5. <u>Which is the largest shop at Disneyland?</u> D. The Emporium. This shop is located on prime real estate on Town Square, making it convenient for both those entering and leaving the Park. Over the years, the Emporium has slowly expanded, taking over nearly the entire building on southwest Main Street. Former tenants in space now occupied by the Emporium include the locker area, the Crystal Arcade, and the Candle Shop. But the Emporium is not the only shop to see changes in the 1990s; a false entrance near New Century Timepieces received a mezuzah, a traditional doorpost decoration marking the inhabitants as Jewish.

6. <u>Which is not one of the vehicles that has traveled on Main Street through the years?</u> D. Electric trolley. This is a busy boulevard! Two omnibuses, the two horse-drawn trolleys, the fire engine (the only Main Street vehicle not dreamed up by Walt, but instead by Bob Gurr), a horse-drawn fire wagon, two horse-drawn surreys, two horseless carriages, and Walt's four electric runabouts have all traveled down Main Street at one time or another. However, the surreys and electric cars are not usually seen in today's Disneyland. Bob Gurr, Disneyland's grand master when it comes to vehicles, was given the job of

choosing the colors for the Main Street Vehicles, as well as all the vehicles he designed.

7.   **How is there a little slice of the Burbank Disney Studios on Main Street?** C. Walt's offices from the Disney Studio were meticulously recreated at Disneyland — in 1972, the two offices were packed up entirely (including furniture, even drapes), shipped to Disneyland, and recreated on a new set in 1973 in the Disneyland Opera House. Guests can now see Walt's "Formal" office for visiting dignitaries and celebrities (his "Working" office was sent to Walt Disney World Resort, initially to be part of the "100 Years of Magic" celebration in 2001). Also present is the piano upon which the Sherman Brothers demonstrated many of their creations for Walt's approval.

8.   **What was added to the Disneyland Railroad in 1966?** D. Primeval World Diorama. Like the other Disney-created attractions for the 1964 New York World's Fair, the Magic Skyway found a home at Disneyland. Or rather, some of the prehistoric sets did. Instead of bringing the entire attraction to Disneyland (as with the other attractions which came back to the Park), some of the sets from the Ford exhibit were installed along the train's route, providing a grand finale to a Guest's experience on the Disneyland Railroad. The dinosaurs were part of an exhibit sponsored by the Ford Motor Company, called the Magic Rotunda. Fairgoers were transported past the dinosaurs in Ford cars along the so-called "Magic Skyway." The other possible answers (steam engine, passenger cars, Grand Canyon diorama) did all happen, but much earlier. Guests had complained about feeling like cattle, so rolling stock with passenger seating was a priority in the early years. This was a rare example of Disney theming not fully appealing to the general public in its first attempt.

9.   **Where is the Hotel Marceline?** A. Above the Market House. One of the second story buildings in Main Street proclaims itself to be the Hotel Marceline, in a nod to Walt's hometown as a

boy. It's located at the Market House by the lockers, and offers a wealth of sound effects for the careful listener, including private discussions and the sound of a dentist's drill.

10. <u>What two "arcades" are located on Main Street?</u> C. The Crystal Arcade and the Penny Arcade. Before becoming part of the Emporium, the Crystal Arcade was home to a glassblower and the Book and Candle Shop. The Penny Arcade has seen a few changes since its opening with the Park in 1955, the most recent being the addition of a candy counter (which necessitated the removal of some of the kinetoscopes).

11. <u>Which movie has never run in the Main Street Cinema?</u> B. *The Old Mill*. The Cinema, at 108 Main Street, continuously plays cartoon shorts on six screens: *Steamboat Willie*, *Plane Crazy* (the first Mickey cartoon finished, but the third to be exhibited), *Mickey's Polo Team*, *The Dognapper*, *The Moose Hunt*, and *Traffic Trouble* (a Laurel and Hardy animated featurette). In the early days of Disneyland (until the 1970s, in fact), silent movies from Pearl White or Thomas Edison would play in this theater. The indoor gas lamps were only removed and modernized because of visibility complaints; Walt had really strived for an authentic look and feel. Now, however, the theater plays exclusively Mickey cartoons and is a nice respite from hot days and hectic crowds.

12. <u>How have some cars of the Disneyland Railroad changed since Disneyland first opened?</u> A. Remodeled to passenger cars. When the Santa Fe & Disneyland Limited first began operation, there were also cattle cars and other forms of cars; the idea was to re-create an actual train. Rather than getting into the moment, however, Guests were often annoyed at being treated "like cattle," even if it was meant in fun. The train seating is now varied — one of the trains has forward-facing seats; the rest are side-facing.

13. <u>Throughout the years, which film company has never sponsored a shop on Main Street?</u> D. Fuji. Kodak was an Opening Day

sponsor and remained at Disneyland until 1970. The stores run by GAF and Polaroid were both short-lived, and Kodak returned in 1984 and remains to this day. The Main Street Photo Supply Company (sponsored by Kodak) now occupies the former home of the INA Carefree Corner.

14. <u>What did the Carnation Ice Cream Parlor become in 1997?</u> C. Carnation Café, though the transplanted Blue Ribbon Bakery also took up residence in the former home of Carnation's indoor seating and ice cream fountain. Following an outpouring of fan sentiment, particularly in the form of comments and complaints in person as well as a massive letter-writing (and email-writing) campaign, Disneyland decided not to remove the restaurant entirely or transform it into a different style of service; it retained its table service, but lost the interior seating and soda fountain. Carnation Café is not the first location at Disneyland to be saved by fanmail, letters, and complaints: the Abraham Lincoln attraction faced extinction a few times — first by The Walt Disney Story, which was eventually scaled back to allow for Lincoln to make use of the theater again, and later by MuppetVision 3D, which would eventually find a home in Disney's California Adventure Park.

Section Two - Medium

15. <u>Approximately how long is the Disneyland Railroad track?</u> B. 1.5 miles. In the 1990s we were told in the spiel that the railroads have covered enough track since opening in 1955 to circle the world 150 times, though that number has definitely increased since the spiel was recorded many years prior.

16. <u>What is the name of the statue in the middle of the Central Plaza?</u> D. Partners. To capture the spirit of Walt and Mickey, Walt Disney Imagineering President Marty Sklar contacted retired Imagineer Blaine Gibson, an incredible sculptor who

worked at WED from 1954 until his retirement in 1983. Blaine is responsible for sculpting nearly all of the Park's original Audio-Animatronics, including the Abraham Lincoln figure in the Great Moments with Mr. Lincoln attraction.

17. **Who is the Honorary Mayor of Disneyland, according to a window above City Hall?** F. Jack Lindquist. Jack was the first president of Disneyland, from 1990-1993. Until Jack's tenure, the highest-ranking personnel responsible for the Park were always at a Vice-President level. This custom had gone back to the earliest days of the Park, when a Disneyland Operations Committee ran the property, but were ultimately responsible to Walt Disney.

18. **What is the significance of the electric car formerly on display in the Walt Disney Story exhibit at the Opera House?** B. Walt's guest parade car. He used this surrey whenever he wanted to entertain private guests and drive them around Main Street. In all, four were produced.

19. **What was the original finale music for Great Moments with Mr. Lincoln?** E. "Battle Hymn of the Republic." During this music, the sky behind Mr. Lincoln formed the stars and stripes of the American flag. The second incarnation featured the music "Golden Dream," which originated at Epcot's American Adventure pavilion, and it seemed to capture the softer, gentler approach to Lincoln after the initial burst of patriotism had died down. With the change in music also came a change in the sky, from nighttime to dawn as the finale of the speech neared, with the faint image of an bald eagle appearing in the sky slightly above Lincoln's right shoulder. A new show, introduced in 2001, saw the return of "Battle Hymn of the Republic."

20. **The owl formerly in the Walt Disney Story, at the Opera House, originated from what Disney movie?** F. *So Dear to My Heart.* The schoolteaching owl in the Walt Disney Story lobby (named Y. Zol Owl) presented some clips from True-Life Adventure movies; of particular note is the "Scorpion Square Dance" from

The Living Desert. This sequence was controversial in its time, for it gave critics ample grist for claiming that Walt's "documentaries" were tainted by editing (the clip shows scorpions locked in combat, but plays forwards and backwards in a way that gives the impression of dance). Walt shrugged and claimed that his films entertained as well as educated.

21. **What scale is the Disneyland Railroad?** C. Five-eighths. Because this is the scale of the railroad and the Mark Twain, it is often assumed that all of Disneyland is this scale. That is simply not true; Imagineers in fact just often "eyeball" the scale: whatever looks good, and fits in with the surroundings well, is chosen for the scale.

22. **What kind of music plays on Main Street?** C. Ragtime and showtunes. Musicals are well represented in the diverse selections, including tracks from *The Happiest Millionaire*, *The Music Man*, *Oklahoma!*, and *Hello, Dolly!* Some of the tracks on the current music loop of 29 songs were recorded by Paragon Ragtime Orchestra and installed in 1992, replacing the previous loops (ranging from 15-21 songs, including patriotic selections in the 1970s) which began playing at Disneyland's opening back in 1955.

23. **Who designed the Main Street vehicles?** B. Bob Gurr. Bob was the man responsible for many of the vehicles at Disneyland; he once said that "if it moves on wheels at Disneyland, I probably designed it." His name is mentioned most often in association with the Autopia cars — he's worked on nearly every incarnation of them at Disneyland. The Autopia cars also gave him his start at vehicle design with Disney — while at the Studio one day he explained how he could better the working model of an Autopia car, not realizing that he was in the presence of Walt Disney!

24. **What was the Opera House used for before the Babes in Toyland Exhibit moved in?** D. Lumber mill. Construction chief Joe Fowler realized the importance of having one on site, and

advised immediate construction of one. Roy O. Disney miraculously found the money and it was constructed in December of 1954. It wasn't until 1961 that the building was actually opened to the public to display the *Babes in Toyland* sets. Within two years the sets were gone and the Opera House was the home of the Mickey Mouse Club. Soon after that the Town Square structure would house Great Moments with Mr. Lincoln.

25. **Who sang "Two Brothers" in Great Moments with Mr. Lincoln?** A. Colombian folksinger Alicia Almo. The song, which tells the story of two brothers fighting on opposite sides during the Civil War, used photographs that were recent but appeared authentic. The lyrics to the song as used in the show reinforced the futility of Civil War by tracing one family's tragedy: "One was gentle, one was kind / One came home, one stayed behind / A cannon ball don't pay no mind / A cannon ball don't pay no mind / If you're gentle or if you're kind."

26. **What is the elevation of Disneyland, as given on the Main Street Train Station?** D. 138 feet above sea level. A second elevation sign at the Frontierland Train Station reads 144, indicating a change in elevation of 6 feet.

27. **For whom is Disneyland's fifth train engine named?** C. Ward Kimball. The acquisition of this newest engine (formerly the Maud L.) is a long and interesting story. It begins with a trade made with train collector Bill Norred. In exchange for an unused set of Disneyland train cars, the Park got an engine that would be given to Walt Disney World Resort. However, because of problems relating to the track configuration, this train was never run and instead was traded to Cedar Fair for the Maud L. Like the Fred Gurley, the Maud L. served time on the Mississippi River Sugar Belt Railroad. The decision was made to name this engine after Disney Studio legend and railroad buff Ward Kimball, who was largely responsible for fueling Walt's renewed interest in trains. Even more complicated – that engine

sent to Cedar Fair was briefly christened the Ward Kimball also, but its name was changed when it changed ownership.

Section Three - Difficult

28. <u>What was the original name of the Plaza Inn?</u> Red Wagon Inn. The restaurant takes its name from the logo of the sponsor, Swift. In 1965, Swift ended its sponsorship and the restaurant received a major renovation in a project worked on by legendary Disney Imagineer John Hench.

29. <u>What planned area next to the Market House gave rise to the idea of a talking Confucius head?</u> Chinatown. Walt wanted to put a Chinese restaurant here, complete with a talking, interactive robot of Confucius, who would respond to Guests' questions. Originally, this had meant that an operator would be nearby but hidden, and who would speak into a microphone to make the robot's mouth move to mimic the words coming from it. In the years before animated presidents or even animated birds, this was a Herculean task, and the technology simply was not up to it. Disney Imagineers did learn quite a bit about robots by mocking up a talking Chinese head, however, which they put to use in animating the birds of the Enchanted Tiki Room instead.

30. <u>Town Square Café had three other names during periods when it was hosted by outside companies. What were they?</u> From 1955 until 1957, it was the Maxwell House Coffee House; it became the Hills Brothers Coffee House from 1958-1976. From 1976-1978 it served as the Town Square Café, but then became the American Egg Council's Egg House from 1978-1983. It then became the Town Square Café once again, from 1983 until its closure in 1992. Usually, this restaurant was only open for breakfast, as people tended not to return that far down Main Street during the Park's busy hours. In 1996 and 1997 it was transformed into a tie-in with the live-action version of *101*

Dalmatians, and then served as a center for pin trading activity. The kitchen and access doors from its days as a restaurant are still present, however.

31. **What names has the Kennel had?** It began as the Ken-L-Land Pet Motel in 1958 and stayed that way until 1968, at which point it became Kal Kan's Kennel Club until 1977, and then reverted to a sponsorless Kennel. From 1986-1991 it was Gaines' Pet Care Kennel, and a new sponsor was located in 1993, when it became Friskies Kennel Club. The Kennel usually caters to cats and dogs, as no animals except service animals (such as seeing-eye dogs) are allowed inside the Park, but will take any non-poisonous animal brought along – they have cared for snakes and monkeys, for example. The Kennel even has its own fire hydrant for the dogs brought out to stretch their legs!

32. **Which speeches of Abraham Lincoln's did we hear in Great Moments with Mr. Lincoln until 2001?** The speech that the Audio-Animatronics Abraham Lincoln gave in the attraction was actually a mixture of four different speeches the 16th president gave both before and during his two terms in the White House. The excerpts and the order they were used in are as follows: Address at Sanitary Fair (1864); Speech at Edwardsville, Illinois (1858); Address of the Young Men's Lyceum in Springfield, Illinois (1838); Address at Cooper Institute (1860).

33. **Who became the voice of Abraham Lincoln when the attraction was altered to show a single speech at Gettysburg?** Warren Burton. Until the 2001 changeover to a new attraction, Royal Dano provided the voice of Lincoln. Royal's voice was also used for a Lincoln voiceover in the Circle-Vision film "American Journeys," and for Walt Disney World Resort's "Hall of Presidents" attraction. The face of Lincoln, interestingly enough, is accurate; it was taken from a life-mask made in 1860 during Lincoln's lifetime. Disney sculptor Blaine Gibson was responsible for creating the incredible likeness of Lincoln.

34. **Which sponsors on Main Street have been there since Park opening?** Carnation (Carnation Café), and Coca-Cola (Refreshment Corner) are the two remaining Main Street participants from Opening Day still at Disneyland.

35. **How is "forced perspective" utilized on Main Street?** It makes the buildings seem taller. Forced perspective is a trick often used in filmmaking; objects which are further away appear smaller, so intentionally reducing the size of an object makes it appear further away. On Main Street, the first floor is about 9/10ths scale, the second floor 8/10ths and the third floor about 7/10ths.

36. **What did the Kalamazoo Manufacturing Company give to Walt, who promptly installed it in Disneyland?** The Handcar visible outside the Main Street Train Station. The handcar came from Kalamazoo, and rests on an adjacent track.

37. **Who painted the slides for the original Great Moments with Mr. Lincoln presentation?** Sam McKim. The original slideshow build-up to the Audio-Animatronics figure was a presentation telling the story of Lincoln's life, narrated by "Lincoln" himself. In 1984 the attraction was refurbished and the slideshow was changed to depict the Civil War. Sam's original drawings were on display in the lobby of the Disneyland Opera House for many years.

38. **What are the origins of the model of the U.S. Capitol building in Great Moments with Mr. Lincoln?** This model, scaled to 3/16th of an inch per foot, was carved from caenstone by French sculptor George Lloyd in 1932. He had given it to Walt in 1962 just before his death, for inclusion in Disneyland, and it was installed at the Opera House as part of the attraction's original prologue in 1965.

Tomorrowland

Tomorrowland Questions

Section One - Easy

1. What is the name of the video game arcade in Tomorrowland?
   a. Starcade
   b. StarQuest
   c. DisneyQuest
   d. Spacecade

2. What served as the icon for Tomorrowland when Disneyland first opened?
   a. Space Mountain
   b. Submarine Voyage
   c. Rocket Jets
   d. Moonliner

3. What attraction did the Rocket Rods replace?
   a. PeopleMover
   b. Viewliner
   c. Submarine Voyage
   d. Tron Light-Cycles

4. What was the name of the interactive fountain in front of *Honey, I Shrunk the Audience?*
    a. Stellar Water
    b. Future Fountain
    c. Cosmic Waves
    d. Astro Beach

5. What attraction has <u>not</u> been housed in the revolving carousel building in Tomorrowland?
    a. Carousel of Progress
    b. Primeval World
    c. Innoventions
    d. America Sings

6. What was the occasion celebrated by the opening of America Sings?
    a. American Bicentennial
    b. Jimmy Carter's presidential election
    c. American man on the moon
    d. Opening of the Rock & Roll Hall of Fame

7. What is the Observatron?
    a. The security observation booth on the roof of Star Tours
    b. The video-monitoring system in Star Tours
    c. The rising stage at Club Buzz

d. The kinetic sculpture atop the former Rocket Rods load platform

8. Who was <u>not</u> one of Captain EO's shipmates?
    a. Hooter
    b. Major Domo
    c. Fuzzball
    d. Rex

9. What song was created for Adventure Thru Inner Space?
    a. "Miracles From Molecules"
    b. "Miracles From the Atom"
    c. "Mysteries of the Mighty Eye"
    d. "Mysteries of the Molecules"

10. Who was the primary America Sings host, present in every scene?
    a. Swanson
    b. Sam
    c. Billy
    d. Pancho

11. What was the defining feature of the Monsanto House of the Future?
    a. It had no windows
    b. It had a glass ceiling
    c. It was made entirely of plastic
    d. An actual family lived there

12. What was the Supreme Leader's last line of defense in *Captain EO?*
    a. Whip Warriors
    b. Supreme Warriors
    c. Supreme Guards
    d. Republican Guards

13. On the PeopleMover, what was in the SuperSpeed Tunnel?
    a. Racing footage and excerpts from the movie *Tron*
    b. Lights arcing overhead like electrons
    c. Laser-shooting villains
    d. A glimpse of Space Mountain in the dark

14. What was the name of the conveyance system used in Adventure Thru Inner Space?
    a. Atomobiles
    b. Atomcarts
    c. Atomboats
    d. Atommovers

15. What was the name of the popular cheeseburgers at the Tomorrowland Terrace before it switched to a healthier menu in the 1990s?
    a. Saturn Burgers
    b. Mars Burgers

    c. Moon Burgers

    d. Venus Burgers

16. What were the futuristic bumper cars in Tomorrowland called?

    a. Astro Bumpers

    b. Cosmic Cars

    c. Hover Cars

    d. Flying Saucers

17. What did the Clock of the World do?

    a. Displayed California time on a globe background

    b. Displayed local time for five time zones spread across world

    c. Displayed local time for all continents

    d. Displayed local time in each time zone

18. How many PeopleMover cars were linked in a train?

    a. Three

    b. Four

    c. Five

    d. Six

19. Who was Captain EO's superior officer, seen via hologram?

    a. Commander Maugh

    b. Commander Bog

c. Commander Murtaugh

d. Commander Mauve

20. What rocket type provided the model for the Rocket Jets?
    a. Jupiter
    b. Titan
    c. Atlas
    d. Saturn

21. What kind of molecule did we approach and penetrate in Adventure Thru Inner Space?
    a. Water
    b. Gasoline
    c. Salt
    d. Carbon dioxide

22. What did we see at the finale of Adventure Thru Inner Space that was both a little unsettling and funny?
    a. Ourselves
    b. Other riders being shrunk
    c. A giant eye
    d. Hitchhiking Ghosts

23. What is the name of the reporter in the queue video for *Honey, I Shrunk the Audience*?
    a. Stacey Jackson
    b. Ian Holmes

c. Jan Greenfield

d. Nigel Channing

24. What did Crazy Larry sell?
   a. Moon rocks
   b. Fashion accessories
   c. Web site hosting
   d. Used satellites and spaceships

25. What crisis in the Mission to Mars show prompted a premature return to earth?
   a. Meteor shower
   b. Comet strike
   c. Fuel leak
   d. Solar flares

26. What was the Grand Canyon Diorama's claim to fame when it opened?
   a. World's first diorama
   b. World's longest diorama
   c. First Disneyland attraction to open after the Park's Grand Opening
   d. First Disneyland attraction dedicated by Richard Nixon

27. What was the spaceship above the Space
    Mountain loading zone identified as?
    a. The Discoverer
    b. Disneyland Starship
    c. Disneyland CMB
    d. DL2000
    e. DL3000
    f. X-1

28. Where besides Innoventions is Tom
    Morrow mentioned?
    a. Star Tours
    b. Submarine Voyage
    c. Rocket Rods
    d. Space Mountain
    e. *American Journeys*
    f. Tomorrowland Autopia

29. Which was <u>not</u> one of the nine tongue-in-
    check "proposed stops" for future
    expansion of the Rocket Rods, as was seen
    in the attraction's queue?
    a. Disney's California Adventure
    b. The beach
    c. The mall
    d. The mountains
    e. The airport
    f. Hollywood

30. What was the top speed of the Rocket Rods?
    a. 20 m.p.h.
    b. 25 m.p.h.
    c. 30 m.p.h.
    d. 35 m.p.h.
    e. 40 m.p.h.
    f. 45 m.p.h.

31. How many unique film presentations appeared in the Rocket Rods queue (formerly the Circle-Vision theater) before the cycle repeated?
    a. One
    b. Two
    c. Three
    d. Four
    e. Five
    f. Six

32. In Star Tours, what are the call signs for the two X-Wings which follow the leader and accompany our shuttle into the run at the Death Star's trench?
    a. Red-24 and Red-26
    b. Red-26 and Blue-30
    c. Red-24 and Red-30
    d. Blue-24 and Blue-30
    e. Blue-26 and Blue-30
    f. Blue-24 and Blue-26

33. What is the current version ("Mark") of the Disneyland monorails?
    a. Mark II
    b. Mark III
    c. Mark IV
    d. Mark V
    e. Mark VI
    f. Mark VII

34. What was the Delta-sponsored animated lion named in the Circle-Vision pre-show?
    a. Leonard the Lion
    b. Leopold the Lion
    c. Lucky the Lion
    d. Delta the Lion
    e. Dennis the Delta Air Lion
    f. Dusty the Delta Air Lion

35. What role does Eric Idle play at the Imagination Institute?
    a. Dr. Neville Channing
    b. Dr. Nigel Channing
    c. Jan Greenfield
    d. Wayne Szalinski
    e. Nick Szalinski
    f. Nameless technician

36. Who was not one of the original participants of Innoventions?
    a. Kaiser
    b. AT&T
    c. Honeywell

d. SAP

e. Nokia

f. General Motors

37. What attraction had the Park's first "speedramp"?

    a. Space Mountain

    b. Starcade

    c. Tomorrowland Train Station

    d. Monorail

    e. PeopleMover

    f. Rocket Jets

38. What company constructed the Flying Saucers?

    a. Walt Disney Imagineering

    b. Cedar Fair

    c. Arrow Development

    d. B & M

    e. Custom Coasters Inc.

    f. General Electric

39. What attraction heralded the advent of E-Tickets?

    a. Monorail

    b. Submarine Voyage

    c. Matterhorn Bobsleds

    d. Space Mountain

    e. Adventure Thru Inner Space

    f. Autopia

40. Besides the House of the Future, what early Tomorrowland exhibit did Monsanto sponsor?
   a. Bathroom of Tomorrow
   b. Tomorrowland Art Corner
   c. Flight Circle
   d. Hall of Chemistry
   e. Hall of Aluminum
   f. Space Station X-1

41. What Tomorrowland attraction first appeared at the 1964-65 New York World's Fair?
   a. Space Mountain
   b. Rocket Jets
   c. Carousel of Progress
   d. Circle-Vision
   e. Adventure Thru Inner Space
   f. Star Tours

42. What were the first words in Adventure Thru Inner Space you heard once seated in your vehicle?
   a. "For centuries, man has searched for small objects"
   b. "For centuries, man sought to find the atom"
   c. "For centuries, man had but his own two eyes"
   d. "For centuries, man could not see microscopic objects"

e. "For centuries, man yearned to see at the molecular level"
f. "For centuries, man tried to perfect the microscope"

43. Which of these was <u>not</u> one of the six characters you could call on the phones in the Premiere Shop's "Kiddie Phones," at the exit to Circle-Vision?
    a. Snow White
    b. Grumpy
    c. Dopey
    d. Donald
    e. Jiminy Cricket
    f. Goofy

44. Which American decade was <u>not</u> represented in the original Carousel of Progress show?
    a. 1900s
    b. 1920s
    c. 1940s
    d. 1960s
    e. 1980s

45. What artist designed the murals that were installed for the 1967 Tomorrowland?
    a. Peter Ellenshaw
    b. Marc Davis
    c. Claude Coats
    d. Herb Ryman

e. Mary Blair

f. Ken Anderson

46. Which is <u>not</u> one of the four eras of American music that comprised the America Sings acts?

    a. Old West

    b. Deep South

    c. Dixieland Jazz

    d. Roaring Twenties

    e. Urban City

47. Which of the following was <u>not</u> one of the Circle-Vision movies at Disneyland?

    a. *A Tour of the West*

    b. *America from Above*

    c. *America the Beautiful*

    d. *American Journeys*

    e. *Wonders of China*

48. Disney artist Peter Ellenshaw was art director for which film?

    a. *A Tour of the West*

    b. *America from Above*

    c. *America the Beautiful*

    d. *American Journeys*

    e. *Wonders of China*

    f. *Magic Journeys*

49. Who directed *Captain EO*?

    a. George Lucas

    b. Steven Spielberg

c. Stanley Kubrick

d. Francis Ford Coppola

e. Terence Malick

f. Quentin Tarantino

50. What model number is the Star Speeder you fly on while riding Star Tours?
    a. 1000
    b. 2000
    c. 3000
    d. 4000
    e. XPR 2000
    f. XPR 3000

51. What refrigerator company originally sponsored Circarama?
    a. General Electric
    b. Whirlpool
    c. Amana
    d. Kelvinator
    e. Kenmore
    f. Traulsen

52. What year was Tomorrowland originally supposed to represent?
    a. 1966
    b. 1976
    c. 1986
    d. 1996
    e. 2006
    f. 2055

53. In what year was the monorail expanded to the Disneyland Hotel?
   a. 1961
   b. 1962
   c. 1963
   d. 1964
   e. 1965
   f. 1966

54. What was on the second floor of the Carousel of Progress?
   a. Walt's offices
   b. Corporate exhibits
   c. The American Home exhibit
   d. The Home of the Future exhibit
   e. Progress City model
   f. Tomorrowland attraction blueprints

55. What was the monorail's claim to fame when it opened in 1959?
   a. First monorail in the world
   b. First daily operating monorail in the world
   c. Fastest monorail in the world
   d. Monorail with longest track in the world
   e. First monorail in Western Hemisphere ever
   f. First daily operating monorail in Western Hemisphere

56. How is the submarine dry-dock camouflaged?

57. What is the monorail's nickname?

58. What themes were originally considered for the Tomorrowland pizza eatery before settling on Redd Rockett's Pizza Port?

59. What companies have sponsored the Autopia?

60. What is the history of the kinetic sculpture atop the Astro Orbitor?

61. What are the names of the family members shown in the Carousel of Progress?

62. How are the vehicles on the Astro Orbitor identified?

63. What water-based attraction preceded the Submarine Voyage in the Tomorrowland Lagoon?

64. What Circle-Vision film debuted at the 1958 Brussels' World's Fair?

65. What was the family dog named in the Carousel of Progress?

66. Who made the C-3PO and R2-D2 droids for the queue area of Star Tours?

67. What were the names of the space cabins in Rocket to the Moon?

68. What ride made use of a World War II German artillery gun?

69. By 1956, the entrance to Tomorrowland was marked by the "Avenue of the Flags." Where were these flags originally located in Disneyland?

70. Where did Walt find the monorail technology?

71. What did the Art Corner sell?

72. Who sponsored the Hall of Aluminum in 1955?

73. Who performed the Space Mountain onboard soundtrack?

74. What Disneyland expansion that never occurred led Walt to explore a partnership with General Electric and the 1964

World's Fair, culminating in the Carousel of Progress?

75. What were the names of the eight Disneyland submarines?

76. What real-life event inspired Disneyland's Submarine Voyage?

77. In 1955, what eatery occupied the space now home to the monorail platform?

78. What type of engine was used to power the Viewliner?

79. Who was the original "sponsor" of Space Mountain?

80. What radio station does Star Tours' labor-avoiding droid G29T listen to during the Sector Two portion of the queue?

81. Where did the Imagineers find the Calamarian for the security booth in the overflow section of the Star Tours queue?

82. What did Space Station X-1 change its name to?

83. Who composed the orchestral score for the queue in the Rocket Rods?

Tomorrowland Answers

Section One - Easy

1. <u>What is the name of the video game arcade in Tomorrowland?</u>
A. Starcade. Like most arcades, this one charges coins (not included with admission) and updates its games regularly. Several new designs for games have been introduced here; the R360 game, which spins players in a gyroscope as they control a fighter jet, and Aladdin VR are two such examples. In 1999 the second level of the arcade was cleared away and closed to the public, leaving some Disneyland Guests upset at the loss of the air hockey tables and pinball machines.

2. <u>What served as the icon for Tomorrowland when it first opened?</u> D. Moonliner. Originally sponsored by TWA, it became the Douglas Moonliner in 1962. In the days before the Matterhorn or Space Mountain, this tall monument served as the icon many families first noticed on their way to Disneyland. In the 1998 redesign of Tomorrowland, a replica of the Moonliner was again constructed from original plans, but the tall mountain ranges of today's Disneyland easily dwarf the rocket, which is only 2/3 its original size. Then, the Moonliner was just a monument in front of Rocket to the Moon, an attraction also sponsored by TWA and then Douglas; today, it marks the spot for one of the best-themed vending areas in Disneyland. As the logo states, it is there "Delivering Refreshment to a Thirsty Galaxy."

3. <u>What attraction did the Rocket Rods replace?</u> A. The PeopleMover. The Rocket Rods streaked along the same raised concrete pathways that the PeopleMover had traveled, though

at a considerably faster rate. The computerized technology that made the Rods possible originated in Walt Disney World Resort, with the GM-sponsored Test Track.

4. **What was the name of the interactive fountain in front of** *Honey, I Shrunk the Audience?* C. Cosmic Waves. At the time of opening, this fountain was the largest of its kind in the world, featuring 201 "Hydro Jets" arranged in three concentric circles. In the middle of it all was a solid granite ball, weighing 12,700 pounds and requiring 16 psi of pressure to lift it off its base. The fountain was programmed by David Durham, who also programmed the troop transports in the Indiana Jones Adventure in Adventureland.

5. **What attraction has not been housed in the revolving carousel building in Tomorrowland?** B. The Primeval World. The Carousel of Progress (1967-1973), America Sings (1974-1988), and Innoventions (1998-) have all been in the carousel building at one time or another. The Carousel of Progress went on to Walt Disney World Resort, while Innoventions originated in Walt Disney World Resort in a non-revolving format.

6. **What was the occasion celebrated by the opening of America Sings?** A. The American Bicentennial celebration in 1976. The patriotic fervor sweeping the nation was captured by Disney in the parade "America on Parade" and the Disneyland-only show America Sings, which celebrated American music through the ages. Oddly enough, the original sponsor of America Sings was Del Monte – though not until 1978.

7. **What is the Observatron?** D. The kinetic sculpture atop the former Rocket Rods load platform. The Observatron is actually the structure that was formerly the Rocket Jets, converted into a kinetic sculpture that briefly comes to life every fifteen minutes — it spins, raises and lowers its satellite-dish-encrusted arms, and shines colored lights while accompanied by uplifting music. The use of the old Rocket Jet superstructure illustrates one principle of Disneyland construction — never get rid of

something that might be useful. The Observatron is meant to provide a "communal square" for the land, with the music tracks culled from the movies *Iron Will* (music by Joel McNeely), *The Rocketeer* (music by James Horner), and from two Disneyland Paris attractions: the Visionarium Timekeeper show (music by Bruce Broughton) and the onboard soundtrack from the Paris Space Mountain (music by Steve Bramson).

8. <u>Who was not one of Captain EO's shipmates?</u> D. Rex. Rex is our pilot onboard the Star Speeder 3000 in Star Tours. In *Captain EO*, the flying rodent was named Fuzzball, the elephant-like blue klutz was Hooter, the furry creatures joined Siamese-style were Idee and Odee, and the robot combination was Major Domo and Minor Domo.

9. <u>What song was created for Adventure Thru Inner Space?</u> A. "Miracles From Molecules." This song, written by Richard and Robert Sherman, combines the happy Disney vision of the future with Monsanto's products: "Every atom is a world / An infinity unfurled / A world of inner space without an end / A world of mystery / Of endless energy / With treasures more than man can ever spend!"

10. <u>Who was the primary America Sings host, present in every scene?</u> B. Sam. This bald eagle (voiced by Burl Ives), and his companion, an owl named Ollie, are in every scene and are our ostensible hosts. A strong argument could also be made for the weasel, who pops out of a barrel or window in each set. The barbershop quartet of geese are also in each major scene, but not at the introduction or conclusion.

11. <u>What was the defining feature of the Monsanto House of the Future?</u> C. It was made entirely of plastic. Located in Alpine Gardens between Tomorrowland and Fantasyland, it had four modules designed by MIT and such innovations as a microwave oven, an ultrasonic dishwasher, climate control, push-button and memory-dialing telephones and telescreen communications. It was updated twice in its ten-year history, and it is

commemorated in today's Tomorrowland along the exterior of Innoventions' Home Zone. Interestingly, the House of the Future even played a role in the Cold War politics of one-upmanship; in 1962 the Soviet Union announced the creation of "the world's first plastic house." Trouble was, Disneyland's version had been around since 1957, and the Soviets, when pressed, produced a photo of Russian diplomats visiting what was clearly the Monsanto prototype.

12. <u>What was the Supreme Leader's last line of defense in *Captain EO*?</u> A. Whip Warriors. She calls for them after EO has transformed her legions of soldiers and approaches her — still on foot — and they emerge from their cybernetic niches in the columns that flank her. EO's friend Fuzzball confounds their whips, however, and EO is able to transform them as well.

13. <u>On the PeopleMover, what was in the SuperSpeed Tunnel?</u> A. Racing footage and excerpts from the movie *Tron*. This section of the PeopleMover was installed in 1977 after Progress City was removed from the top level of the Carousel of Progress, and the area was sealed off into a tunnel. Projectors and large screens created an ideal way to simulate fast movement, aided by low-tech fans along the floor. The first film shown was race cars along a race track, part of a five-sequence loop that also included water skiing, motorcycles, and an air boat. After the 1982 premiere of *Tron*, sequences from the movie were installed in place of the racing.

14. <u>What was the name of the conveyance system used in Adventure Thru Inner Space?</u> A. Atomobiles. The system as a whole is called the Omnimover system, though these cars in this particular attraction were called Atomobiles. Like all Omnimovers, these were controlled by a 12-volt electric drive train that moved all cars at once. Individual motion of each car, however, allowed designers to rotate up to 180 degrees and control precisely what the guests looked at. The sound system, heard via three speakers in each car, was transmitted at odd-

numbered cars, then projected to the even-numbered car directly behind it.

15. **What was the name of the popular cheeseburgers at the Tomorrowland Terrace before it switched to a healthier menu in the 1990s?** C. Moon Burgers. Sponsored by Coke, the Terrace replaced the Yacht Bar (formerly Yacht Club) in the new Tomorrowland of 1967 and with its descending stage quickly became one of the dance venues at the Park. The inclusion of Space Mountain in 1977 to Tomorrowland served to re-energize the space theme of the area, and the addition of the Space Place Restaurant near Space Mountain also occasioned the theming of the Tomorrowland Terrace menu into futuristic items such as the Moon Burgers. Menu theming can of course be found throughout Disneyland's history; the Village Haus, for example, offered the Toymaker (bacon cheeseburger) and the Puppeteer (chicken salad), while the Character Food stands which predated the Village Haus served Nottingham Burgers and Sherwood Franks.

16. **What were the futuristic bumper cars in Tomorrowland called?** D. Flying Saucers. These Guest favorites were constantly having mechanical difficulties, and were finally removed in 1966, after only five years at Disneyland. They stood roughly where the Imagination Institute is now located.

17. **What did the Clock of the World do?** D. Displayed local time in each time zone. It could tell the time throughout the world (hence its name), but only if you knew how to compare the various symbols along the clock face. A map of the world was broken down into 24 sections, which corresponded to 24 moving numbers along the clock's top rim. To determine the minutes, a Guest would need to read a small ball near the top of the display.

18. **How many PeopleMover cars were linked in a train?** B. Four. The primary colors on the PeopleMover were red, yellow, dark blue and aqua. To achieve a more futuristic look and to mesh

better with the largely white-colored Tomorrowland, they were repainted white in the 1980s, but kept colored stripes along the middle.

19. **Who was Captain EO's superior officer, seen via hologram?** B. Commander Bog. He was played by Dick Shawn (1929-1987), a character actor in Hollywood since the 1960s. One of his last roles was in the 1987 movie *Maid to Order* as Stan Starkey. Anjelica Huston played the Supreme Leader, while Debbie Lee Carrington, Tony Cox, and Gary Depew lent their voices as Idee, Hooter, and Major Domo, respectively.

20. **What rocket type provided the model for the Rocket Jets?** D. Saturn. The Rocket Jets revolved around a Saturn-type rocket, which, with its multiple boosters, is recognizable as the rocket series responsible for making the only manned missions to the moon.

21. **What kind of molecule did we approach and penetrate in Adventure Thru Inner Space?** A. Water. Specifically, we approached a snowflake, so the first sets were large-sized snowflakes that got ever larger as we continued to "shrink." Finally we saw the molecules themselves, separated from each other, covered by rapidly spinning electronics in perhaps the neatest effect of the attraction. We got closer still, down to the atomic level, at which point our host panicked and brought us back to our normal size. If one were to look closely at the arrangement of the two hydrogen and one oxygen atom, one could even make out a hidden Mickey Mouse shape, said by some to be the first intentional "Hidden Mickey" in Disney theme park history. Many would follow in the years to come.

22. **What did we see at the finale of Adventure Thru Inner Space that was both a little unsettling and funny?** C. A giant eye. As the mission commander brought us back to normal size, he verified that we'd returning by locating us through his microscope. From our perspective, we saw his giant eye, gazing penetratingly — and disconcertingly — at each of us in turn.

23. What is the name of the reporter in the queue video for *Honey, I Shrunk the Audience*? C. Jan Greenfield. The "World News Network" correspondent is interviewing the Imagination Institute's Stacey Jackson (the one person at the Institute who seems to know what she's doing!).

24. What did Crazy Larry sell? D. Used satellites and spaceships. He was visible in the queue video for Space Mountain, and appeared multiple times during commercial interruptions of the supposed broadcast. One of the used vehicles Larry offered was the spaceship from Disney's 1986 movie *Flight of the Navigator*. Crazy Larry was far from the only inside joke or reference; among others, a sign in the queue passageway announced the Spaceport – a reference to Walt's original concept for Space Mountain (then called Spaceport) in 1964.

25. What crisis in the Mission to Mars show prompted a premature return to earth? A. Meteor Shower. This unexpected event prompted our captain to enter hyperspace and quickly return to earth: "Ladies and gentlemen, our camera ship has been knocked out of control by a shower of meteoric particles, we may encounter the same conditions" he said, and when told we received damage, he declared an emergency jump to warp.

26. What was the Grand Canyon Diorama's claim to fame when it opened? B. World's longest diorama. It was also the largest, at 305 feet long and 45 feet wide. It cost over $350,000 and took 80,000 man hours to create, and was opened with a ceremony that featured Walt and 96-year old Hopi Indian Chief Nevangnewa. The opening also marked the debut of engine #3 (Fred Gurley), which had been a working train on a Louisiana sugar plantation before its purchase and retrofitting by Disney. The idea for the canyon came from the 1958 Disney film *Grand Canyon*, which won an Academy Award for short subject. Imagineer Claude Coats, known for his backgrounds on Disney animated features, contributed to the layout of the diorama.

Section Two - Medium

27. <u>What was the spaceship above the Space Mountain loading zone identified as?</u> E. DL3000, though until April 2002 it was labeled as DL2000. The individual pods that made up the long "neck" of the craft were labeled CMB2000. At Walt Disney World Resort, the equivalent ship (which is visible as you are in your trains and ascending for the ride) was named XL2000, but the new sponsor FedEx has renamed it FX-2000. The Disneyland Park spaceship had astronaut figures in its control room, but they were seldom noticed because the ship was so close to the ceiling and the figures were not well lit.

28. <u>Where besides Innoventions is Tom Morrow mentioned?</u> A. Star Tours. The "terminal announcements" state: "Mr. Morrow, Mr. Tom Morrow, please check with a Star Tours agent at gate number four."

29. <u>Which was not one of the nine tongue-in-check "proposed stops" for future expansion of the Rocket Rods, as was seen in the attraction's queue?</u> C. The mall. Future stops that were listed included the mountains, the Disney Studios, Hollywood, the Disneyland Hotel, Disney's California Adventure Park, the beach, the airport, a hockey arena, and a baseball stadium. The sports arena listings on the faux chart were a nod to Disney's ownership at that time of the Anaheim Angels and the Mighty Ducks of Anaheim.

30. <u>What was the top speed of the Rocket Rods?</u> B. 30 MPH. The Rocket Rods traveled around the 4,500 foot-long track at a top speed of exactly 30.68 MPH, making it one of the fastest in-park wheeled vehicle in the Park's history (the monorail is capable of higher speeds, but outside the Park's boundaries; Splash Mountain, which reaches speeds up to 40 MPH briefly, is a flume ride). Each vehicle weighed about 5,600 pounds and was powered by a 200 horsepower electric motor.

31. How many unique film presentations appeared in the Rocket Rods queue (formerly the Circle-Vision theater) before the cycle repeated? C. Three. Besides the Walt Disney Story film at the Opera House, these films featured the only footage of Walt in the Park. Using moments from the long history of Circle-Vision films (dating back to 1955), the presentations were designed to entertain Guests as they wound their way through the former theater, and the cycle of the three segments repeated every few minutes.

32. In Star Tours, what are the call signs for the two X-Wings which follow the leader and accompany our shuttle into the run at the Death Star's trench? C. Red-24 and Red-30. "Red-24, Red-30, cover me, I'm going in," then again later, "Red-24, Red-30, follow me." Our pilot Rex then proclaims that he's "always wanted to do this," but is so excited that he's looking at the audience rather than where he's going, and we almost collide with another X-Wing. The backstory to Star Tours is a bit muddled. Ostensibly, our journey takes place after the rebels have defeated the Emperor and overthrown the Empire. The new galactic order seeks economic revitalization in the form of tourists, travelling to former hot spots such as Endor. However, this does not explain the presence of Imperial forces or yet another Death Star, though arguably these are just the final remnants of the old order, ready to be swept away. When it opened in 1987, Star Tours featured the first video footage of the *Star Wars* universe officially sanctioned by Lucasfilm since the original trilogy had been released.

33. What is the current version ("Mark") of the Disneyland Monorails? D. Mark V. The beloved, and most recognizable design, was the Mark III, with the bubble top in the first car, from which the train was driven (the Mark IV trains are used only at the Walt Disney World Resort).

34. What was the Delta-sponsored animated lion named in the Circle-Vision pre-show? F. Dusty the Delta Air Lion. The pre-show included primitive wall animations representing America

and its various activities around the country, and a cartoon featuring Dusty, as well as another character named Wilbur the Bear, explaining how the show worked. Delta, which had had a partnership with Disney as the official airline, was not the first airline to sponsor Circle-Vision, however — that distinction goes to PSA (whose pre-show mascot had been the albatross Orville in an original film "All Because Man Wanted to Fly" that combined live action and animation).

35. <u>What role does Eric Idle play at the Imagination Institute?</u> B. Dr. Nigel Channing. As the story goes, Channing's grandfather inherited vast sums of money from his inventive father and went on to open the Institute. The legacy of running the institute was first handed down to Nigel's father, Neville, and then to Nigel himself.

36. <u>Who was not one of the original participants of Innoventions?</u> E. Nokia. Compaq (which was featured on the entire lower level), SAP, General Motors, Honeywell, Kaiser, AT&T, and Disney were the original participants. The concept of the attraction is to showcase new technologies that would be constantly updated — a vision brought over from Epcot in Florida. The General Motors exhibit was perhaps the most interesting to Disneyland Park Guests as it was a ride in itself and featured a "minimatronic" by the name of "General Sparky Motors."

37. <u>What attraction had the Park's first "speedramp"?</u> D. The Disneyland monorail, which opened in 1959. In fact, on park maps the speedramps were themselves labeled as if they were an attraction; Guests seeking the "Steven Adamson Speedramps" instead found themselves in line for the monorail! This alternative to escalators also made it easier for wheelchairs to ascend to the platform. Walt envisioned a "world on the move" for Tomorrowland, possibly featuring a second level, with such speedramps shuttling people to the popular attractions quickly and while giving them a rest. Ramps were later installed at the

PeopleMover, Space Mountain, and the Starcade, and horizontal versions of the speedramp now occupy many airports.

38. **What company constructed the Flying Saucers?** C. Arrow Development. The technology for this unique attraction did not really exist in 1961, but Walt did not let that stop him. Giant fans below the surface forced air up through tiny holes in the surface, lifting up the vehicles and allowing Guests, by virtue of leaning in one direction, to zoom off and bounce off of other saucers. The ride was dangerous to work, had low capacity (despite having two arenas to decrease delay caused by loading), and worst of all suffered constant breakdown, usually due to harmonic interference (imbalances in the flow of air upward might reach a threshold, and the whole system would turn off). Such a system now could be greatly improved via the use of computerization, but it would be prohibitively expensive to run the fans.

39. **What attraction heralded the advent of E-Tickets?** B. Submarine Voyage. This attraction opened in 1959 and remained an E-Ticket adventure until the advent of the "passport" in 1981, when all attractions became accessible for one price paid at the front gate (interestingly, the ticket system did not stop until a year later in 1982). There had been only "A" through "D" tickets in Disneyland before the 1959 rehab of the border between Tomorrowland and Fantasyland, which saw the introduction of the Monorail, the Submarine Voyage, and the Matterhorn Bobsleds. The Submarine Voyage opened on June 6, eight days before the other new attractions in the region, making it the first-ever E-Ticket attraction.

40. **Besides the House of the Future, what early Tomorrowland exhibit did Monsanto sponsor?** D. Hall of Chemistry. This exhibit opened with Disneyland in 1955, predating the House of the Future by 2 years. Monsanto would later sponsor Adventure Thru Inner Space in 1967. The presence of Monsanto, a chemical giant, was a good thematic match with

Tomorrowland's original motto: "Nature creates, man discovers."

41. **What Tomorrowland attraction first appeared at the 1964-65 New York World's Fair?** C. Carousel of Progress. At the fair, it had been sponsored by General Electric and was part of a larger exhibit called "Progressland." Walt brought the entire show back to Disneyland, with the curious result that G.E. products were specifically advertised to Guests of the show for years beyond the fair. Stoves, ovens, and refrigerators open on command as our host sings G.E.'s praises for making our lives easier. Of all the shows at Disneyland that began life at the 1964 World's Fair (which includes "it's a small world," the Primeval World, Great Moments with Mr. Lincoln, and the ride system for the PeopleMover), none was as crassly commercial as the Carousel of Progress. If those other attractions even had sponsors while at Disneyland, their presence was restricted to simple brand-building via the inclusion of their name on the marquee. The Carousel of Progress featured 32 Audio-Animatronics, both human and canine, and is now presented in the Magic Kingdom Park at the Walt Disney World Resort.

42. **What were the first words in Adventure Thru Inner Space you heard once seated in your vehicle?** C. "For centuries, man had but his own two eyes." Paul Frees, who also voiced the Haunted Mansion and the introduction to the original Great Moments with Mr. Lincoln, did the narration on this atomic adventure. The ride narration begins: "For centuries, man had but his own two eyes to explore the wonders of his world. Then he invented the microscope — a mighty eye — and discovered the fantastic universe beyond the limits of his own meager sight. Now your adventure through inner space has begun. Through Monsanto's Mighty Microscope you will travel into the incredible universe found within a tiny fragment of a snowflake. I am the first person to make this fabulous journey; suspended in the timelessness of inner space are the thought waves of my first impressions. They will be our only source of contact once you have passed beyond the limits of normal magnification."

43. **Which of these was not one of the six characters you could call on the phones in the Premiere Shop's "Character Phones," at the exit to Circle-Vision?** C. Dopey. This made sense, because Dopey never seems to talk anyway! The available characters were Snow White, Grumpy, Goofy, Mickey, Donald, Jiminy Cricket and (oddly) the Bell Telephone Operator. The characters display their usual attitudes while teaching phone manners and proper phone safety to the children calling them. Grumpy's spiel, for example, went like this: "Hello! This is Grumpy. Who keeps calling me? I've been trying to call Snow White! But her phone has been busy all day! So I went over there and you know what I found? Dopey had been playing with the phone and he left it off the hook. He knows better than that! You know better than that! Everybody knows better than that! People who play with the phone and leave it off the hook are just plain Dopey. And they make me Grumpy! Good-bye!" This delightful free attraction was sponsored by Bell Telephone and was informally known as the "Small Fry" phones when it premiered in the late 1960s.

44. **Which American decade was not represented in the original Carousel of Progress show?** E. 1980s. Progressland, as it was then called, was conceived for the 1964-65 New York World's Fair, so it was very up to date in setting its scenes in the 1900s, the 1920s, the 1940s, and the 1960s — every twenty years. The show was updated when it moved out to Florida, and eventually jumped from the 1940s to the 1990s, resulting in some dubious life spans for the central family!

45. **What artist designed the murals that were installed for the 1967 Tomorrowland?** E. Mary Blair. Blair was the primary artist and designer on "it's a small world" as well. The mosaic on the south side of Tomorrowland which would later be replaced by a Star Tours mural was not completely lost; remnants of these tile pieces were brought over to Disneyland Resort Paris and installed in a restaurant in their Fantasyland. Very little is thrown away at Disney!

46. **Which is not one of the four eras of American music that comprised the America Sings acts?** C. Dixieland Jazz. Apart from the introduction and closing sequences, which were set in a small-town American local park, the sets were: The Old West (American folk songs), the Deep South (gospel music), the Roaring Twenties (barbershop and other more modern music), and the Urban City (rock and roll).

47. **Which of the following was not one of the Circle-Vision movies at Disneyland?** B. *America from Above. A Tour of the West* (1955-1959), *America the Beautiful* (1960-1984; 1996-1997), *Wonders of China* (1984-1996), and *American Journeys* (1984-1996) were all Circle-Vision films. Originally, the Circarama process used 16mm film and required eleven cameras. By the time a revised *America the Beautiful* debuted in 1967 with a remodeled theater, the rig used for shooting the films weighed 500 pounds, with nine 35-millimeter cameras shooting 40 degrees each of the necessary 360 degrees. These bulky cameras created some unusual shooting problems; for example, one scene of Hawaiian surfers, shot on an outrigger canoe, suffered a dunking in the salty ocean water after the canoe capsized. Filmmakers rushed to create a darkroom right there on the beach, shipped the film home in distilled water, and managed to save the footage, which was later used in *American Journeys*. By 1996 Circle-Vision was on its last legs and about ready to close in preparation for construction on the new Tomorrowland. As a farewell tribute, Park management brought back *America the Beautiful*, which played until Circle-Vision's final night on September 7, 1997.

48. **Disney artist Peter Ellenshaw was art director for which film?** A. *A Tour of the West*. This film was Disney's first attempt at a circular picture show with the Circle-Vision technology, and was a 12-minute tour of the western United States. Peter also contributed to three other early Tomorrowland attractions: Guests viewed his paintings as they rotated around the platform in Space Station X-1, and he helped to create the background for

the 20,000 Leagues Under the Sea Exhibit. Additionally, he contributed to the painting of the Disneyland Spaceport that Guests saw as they blasted off in Rocket to the Moon. His works continue to command much interest in the art world even outside Disney.

49. <u>Who directed *Captain EO*?</u> D. Francis Ford Coppola. George Lucas, who was also working with Walt Disney Imagineering on Star Tours at the time, served as the producer of the 3D film, at the request of star Michael Jackson.

50. <u>What model number is the Star Speeder you fly on while riding Star Tours?</u> C. 3000. This number seemed to function as a subtle continuation of the vehicle numbering system employed elsewhere in Tomorrowland, since the large spaceship hanging in the loading dock of Space Mountain was at the time labeled DL2000; the implication is that the Star Speeder represented the next generation of vehicles in Tomorrowland. In 2002, however, the Space Mountain ship was renamed DL3000, perhaps to maintain a futuristic date (or perhaps to intentionally have the same designation as the Star Speeder).

51. <u>What refrigerator company originally sponsored Circarama?</u> D. Kelvinator. Some people better remember American Motors as the sponsor of Circarama, which makes a bit more sense because most scenes in the early 360-degree films were captured while riding in a car. In fact, the sponsorship was jointly provided by three divisions of American Motors: Kelvinator, Hudson, and Nash.

52. <u>What year was Tomorrowland originally supposed to represent?</u> C. 1986. The original Tomorrowland, according to literature describing it at that time, was made to represent the next passing of Halley's Comet in 1986.

53. <u>In what year was the monorail expanded to the Disneyland Hotel?</u> A. 1961. After two years of serving as just another attraction in Disneyland, in 1961 the Disneyland-Alweg

Monorail System became real transportation and was the first monorail in America to cross a city street (formerly West Street, now Disneyland Drive). In 1986, the American Society of Mechanical Engineers honored the Disneyland monorail by designating it a National Historic Mechanical Engineering landmark.

54. <u>What was on the second floor of the Carousel of Progress?</u> E. Progress City model. This scale model to Walt Disney's envisioned Progress City was the germ of the idea he would soon refine into EPCOT, a prototype community. However, Walt's death caused EPCOT to mutate into a theme park, and it wasn't until the mid-1990s that a city of tomorrow as he had envisioned would appear in the form of Celebration, built on Walt Disney World Resort property. Portions of the Progress City model were moved to the Walt Disney World Resort and are now visible from the Tomorrowland Transportation Authority, Florida's version of the PeopleMover.

55. <u>What was the monorail's claim to fame when it opened in 1959?</u> F. It was the first daily operating monorail in the Western Hemisphere. The opening was attended by Richard Nixon, and when he was whisked off for a pre-ceremony ride by Walt (the monorail was being driven by the ride's designer Bob Gurr), the Secret Service agents were left behind at the station. Walt and Gurr had in effect kidnapped the then vice-president!

Section Three - Difficult

56. <u>How is the submarine dry-dock camouflaged?</u> For years, the dry-dock, which is located behind the Autopia and is visible from the Disneyland Railroad, was partly concealed by a billboard that proclaimed the area to be the "Disneyland Oceanographic Research Institute," as a way to explain the presence of a submarine in the dock. Slightly before the 1998

rehab of Tomorrowland the billboard was eclipsed by a new one which proclaimed "Agrifuture," the notion that all plants used for decoration in the future will be edible.

57. **What is the monorail's nickname?** "Highway in the Sky." This motto was heard on the Disneyland Railroad recorded spiel, as you passed by the monorail track, as well as on the monorail itself. The monorail replaced the Viewliner, but the design of the two trains remained somewhat the same and in fact they had similar track layouts, at least until the monorail was extended to the Disneyland Hotel. Though it was more of a "Viewliner in the Sky," the presence of the Autopia below made the new motto of "Highway in the Sky" irresistible.

58. **What themes were originally considered for the Tomorrowland pizza eatery before settling on Redd Rockett's Pizza Port?** The idea behind Redd Rockett is that he runs an intergalactic pizza chain, with his most recent restaurant opening in Disneyland. But the project first considered several other themes: "Pizza Planet," the *Toy Story* pizza house already found in Disneyland Resort Paris and at Disney-MGM Studios; the "Pan Galactic Pizza Port," an original Imagineering creation already at Tokyo Disneyland Resort; or "Planet Cool," which would have featured old ride vehicles as tables and ceiling decoration (an idea which, while it was not adopted for the eatery, did manage to find life in the Rocket Rods queue and the Premiere Shop, both of which displayed old Tomorrowland ride vehicles).

59. **What companies have sponsored the Autopia?** The original sponsor until 1970 was Richfield Oil, and the sponsor became Chevron in 2000. Richfield used to give out mock paper licenses to children who went on the attraction (an idea continued by Chevron), and there was no center guide rail in those early days. Walt's original idea was to use the Autopia to teach children to drive responsibly on the rapidly spreading freeway system; this is why the layout of the Autopia so closely resembles actual freeways and cloverleafs. Naturally, the children delighted in bumping each other, resulting in much destruction to the

under-protected cars (whose initial bumpers were provided by Kaiser, and were therefore aluminum). The introduction of the guide rail in 1963 went a long way in stopping the destruction, but still many versions of the cars would premiere along the track over the years. The Chevron cars are actually the eighth version, which would make them Mark VIII's.

60. **What is the history of the kinetic sculpture atop the Astro Orbitor?** The Astro Orbitor's design was first worked out for Discoveryland in Disneyland Resort Paris, where it is known as the Orbitron. When plans surfaced for the Tomorrowland rehab at Disneyland, the concept for a spinning ride was redesigned, and the base was built anew at the front of Tomorrowland. The sculpture, which resembles a three-dimensional model of a solar system, was inspired by a set in the 1984 Jim Henson movie *The Dark Crystal*, which in turn had been inspired by medieval models of the solar system. This ties back to the Astro Orbitor's name; Guests are in space (the astros), orbiting around a solar system. Science fiction writer and occasional Imagineering consultant Ray Bradbury contributed to the design of the original Paris design.

61. **What are the names of the family members shown in the Carousel of Progress?** Our host is not named, despite the fact that he does most of the talking! The actor providing his voice was Rex Allen, a narrator in dozens of Disney films and on the various incarnations of "Walt Disney Presents" or "The Wonderful World of Disney." His wife is named Sarah (though he calls her "Mother"), his daughter is named Jane, and the visitor is Uncle Orville (who is probably our host's brother, not his uncle — he tends to refer to family members from the perspective of his children). There is also a grandmother and grandfather (i.e., probably the parents of our host), and a son, who is not given a name either. Rex Allen, who gave the narrator a voice, was also the "voice of Disneyland" during the early years, before Jack Wagner was contracted to perform the parade announcements and safety spiels.

62. **How are the vehicles on the Astro Orbitor identified?** Each rocket on the Astro Orbitor has its own unique symbol, a stylized version of a sign of the zodiac. The idea is to reinforce the mythical futurism found in Jules Verne and the subtle backstory to the current Tomorrowland, that of a nostalgic look at how prior generations conceived of the future.

63. **What water-based attraction preceded the Submarine Voyage in the Tomorrowland Lagoon?** The Tomorrowland Lagoon was first occupied by the Phantom Boats; later, both the Motorboat Cruise and Submarine Voyage took up residence in different parts of the lagoon. The Phantom Boats constantly broke down, and as a result often left the Guests stranded. Sending out an employee on each boat provided a temporary (if cost-ineffective) solution, but something else was needed. The Phantom Boats did make a brief return for the summer of 1956, as nothing had yet been worked out for the Lagoon area, but thereafter they disappeared for the last time.

64. **What Circle-Vision film debuted at the 1958 Brussels' World's Fair?** *America the Beautiful.* This was Disney's second Circle-Vision film, debuting three years after "A Tour of the West." In 1960, the film opened at Disneyland. In 1967, when the Circle-Vision process was revised to utilize 9 cameras instead of 11, the film was re-shot, debuting on June 25, 1967, slightly before the opening of the refurbished Tomorrowland. In 1975 — to commemorate America's Bicentennial — new, patriotic scenes were added. To make way for *Wonders of China* and *American Journeys, America the Beautiful* stopped showing on January 3, 1984, but came back to Disneyland for one final encore just before the Circle-Vision theater closed in September 1997 to be used as the queue for the Rocket Rods. The three most recent Circle-Vision films have been directed by Jeff Blyth.

65. **What was the family dog named in the Carousel of Progress?** In each scene the dog has a new name, presumably because the twenty year jumps between scenes would necessitate getting a new dog! In each case, however, the dog reacted similarly; he

would at one point or another raise his head and bark, eliciting a reproach from his master. It was Walt's idea to add the dog in the show, adding continuity and character to the story. In the 1900s he is called Rover, in the 1920s it is Buster, in the 1940s he is called Sport, and his name is not mentioned in the 1960s. When the show traveled to Walt Disney World Resort, Buster's name was changed to Queenie and the dog in the last scene was named Sport also. After a rehab in the early 1990s, all four dogs were named Rover.

66. **Who made the C-3PO and R2-D2 droids for the queue area of Star Tours?** Lucas' special effects company Industrial Light & Magic (ILM) did, as you might have guessed, but they did not make these robots specifically for Disneyland. These are original movie props! For the movie, there were versions of the droids designed as suits for the actors Kenny Baker (R2-D2) and Anthony Daniels (C-3PO), and there were also fully functional robots; the latter is what we now find in Disneyland. C-3PO's outer skin is covered in gold leaf; no other substance would give off the luster they were seeking. For similar reasons, the spires atop Sleeping Beauty Castle and "it's a small world" are also covered in 22-carat gold leaf, as are some parts of King Arthur Carrousel.

67. **What were the names of the space cabins in Rocket to the Moon?** The original names for the identical cabins – having two of them provided for faster lines and greater capacity – were Luna and Diana, corresponding with the theme of flying to the moon. Soon after opening, the names were changed to Antares and Polaris, the names of two distant stars.

68. **What ride made use of a World War II German artillery gun?** The base of the Astro-Jets, renamed the Tomorrowland Jets in 1964, had used a WWII artillery gun. The ride was an off-the-shelf design from a Bavarian amusement company (the Klaus Company), which had converted the gun into the rotating base. The gun did not form part of the Rocket Jets when the ride was moved to the top of the PeopleMover tower; that ride was built

from the ground up rather than moved, even though it kept the same basic elements as the Astro-Jets. When the Astro Orbitor was constructed in 1998, it was also built completely new, as it was still cheaper to buy a new ride system than to move the existing one.

69. **By 1956, the entrance to Tomorrowland was marked by the "Avenue of the Flags." Where were these flags originally located in Disneyland?** In the middle of Tomorrowland, all 48 flags (this was before Hawaii and Alaska had joined the Union) were crammed into a star design in what was known as the Court of Honor. This location, which was closer to the Tomorrowland Lagoon than to the eventual home of Space Mountain, would soon become the home of the Astro-Jets, so the flags had to be moved to the entrance of Tomorrowland. Extra poles were then added for Hawaii and Alaska.

70. **Where did Walt find the monorail technology?** Walt stumbled across a monorail in Germany, from a company called Alweg, during his frequent travels to Europe in search of amusement park and transportation innovation. Walt briefly considered a "hanging" monorail as the replacement for the down-to-earth — and not very futuristic — Viewliner train, but decided the piggybacked version we have now was a more reliable technology and makes for a less nauseating ride. The Alweg company derived its name from the initials its creator: Dr. Axel Lennart Wenner-Gren.

71. **What did the Art Corner sell?** The Art Corner sold Disney art — cheap — as well as other art supplies and assorted Disneyland keepsakes, such as programs, guidebooks, and postcards. Most tantalizingly, the Art Corner sold production animation cels from Disney movies. While these command thousands of dollars apiece now, they were considered almost worthless at the time, and only key moments from the movies were even considered worthwhile to sell. Most likely the majority of cels here came from *Lady and the Tramp*, the most recent Disney movie at the time, though there a few from *Alice in Wonderland*, *Peter Pan*,

and *Cinderella*. Cels from older Disney movies were mostly destroyed. The Art Corner was located roughly where the Premiere Shop was.

72. <u>Who sponsored the Hall of Aluminum in 1955?</u> Kaiser Aluminum. This exhibit was little more than a corporate advertisement for Kaiser; Guests were welcomed by an all-aluminum mascot named KAP — the Kaiser Aluminum Pig. There was a giant aluminum telescope also near the entrance, while inside was an aluminum time sphere that looked back at how the metal might have been useful throughout history. There had been a talking suit of armor as well, which extolled the virtues of the metal: "I am the Wishful Knight. I wish there had been aluminum in my day! I'd have traded King Arthur's magic sword for some aluminum armor. I'd have been cooler in the heat of battle. My horse and I would have had a lighter load to carry. Free from rust, easy to clean, aluminum would have made me a true knight in shining armor." Kaiser convinced Walt that the bumpers for the soon-to-be-premiered Autopia cars should be made of the "wonder metal" aluminum, but as you might expect, they did very little to protect the cars and they were soon destroyed. The Hall of Aluminum was run by Kaiser, on space leased from Disneyland, so technically it was not required to be open at all times in the day like most of the rides at Disneyland. Kaiser remained in Disneyland until the end of their five-year lease, though they had wanted to leave sooner.

73. <u>Who performed the Space Mountain onboard soundtrack?</u> Dick Dale, best known for his surf guitar music and a particularly "Californian" sound. Through an intricate system of sensors, the soundtrack is synchronized with the ride, so that drops and sudden turns are marked by sudden changes in the music. The opening and closing segments of the soundtrack are adaptations from "Aquarium" in Saint Saens' "Carnevale des Animaux."

74. <u>What Disneyland expansion that never occurred led Disney to explore a partnership with General Electric and the 1964</u>

<u>World's Fair, culminating in the Carousel of Progress?</u> Edison Square, a proposed addition to Main Street, would have examined the role of creativity and invention in American history, much as Greenfield Village had done with Edison and the Wright Brothers. A major inspiration for Edison Square was Thornton Wilder's play "Our Town," which revolved around life in a small American town. Exhibits would have included the American Home, which traced the view of progress through electronics and which would eventually become integrated into the Carousel of Progress, and the Diorama of Inventions, an idea which does not seem to have survived in any form presently at Disneyland. One way to view it is to consider the Carousel of Progress as a fully grown version of the "The American Home," as Imagineers had deemed the idea too good to waste on a small-scale exhibit.

75. **What were the names of the eight Disneyland submarines?**
Though there were only eight subs, there were more than eight names because many were changed when they were painted yellow instead of the original gunmetal gray. However, some of the names repeated themselves, and confusingly, some old names were given to a different sub! Altogether there were thirteen names; here are the ID numbers and the corresponding names: 301 Nautilus (no name change), 302 Triton (new name Neptune), 303 Sea Wolf (new name Sea Star), 304 Skate (new name Explorer), 305 Skipjack (new name Seeker), 306 George Washington (new name Argonaut), 307 Patrick Henry (new name Triton), and 308 Ethan Allen (new name Sea Wolf). The basic idea was to change the military feel to the naming scheme into a more exploratory, research tone.

76. **What real-life event inspired Disneyland's Submarine Voyage?**
A glass-bottomed boat ride was at first considered as a successor to the Phantom Boats in the Tomorrowland Lagoon, but Walt broached the possibility of a "real" submarine ride. Submarines were very much in the public attention in the 1950s, as the world's first nuclear-powered sub, the Nautilus, had launched in 1954 and made its historic first journey under the North Pole in

1958. When the Disneyland Submarine Voyage opened in 1959, it featured, not surprisingly, a journey underneath the North Pole as well. There were also mermaids in the ride, and for a brief time, even live "mermaids" atop the coral reefs out in the lagoon (they were only visible above water, of course). The chlorine would damage their hair, however, and the occasional Guest would jump in to be with the mermaids, so the tactic was soon abandoned.

77. **In 1955, what eatery occupied the space now home to the monorail platform?** The Yacht Club, later renamed Yacht Bar and moved across the way to the current home of Tomorrowland Terrace / Club Buzz. The building was literally picked up intact by a crane and transferred to its new home.

78. **What type of engine was used to power the Viewliner?** A V-8, surprisingly. The entire train, in fact, was manufactured from used car parts, as if to demonstrate the usefulness of recycling wasteful individual transportation systems into a practical mass-transit system. The engine compartment even came complete with a dashboard, which had to have a central section cut out of it to reduce its overall girth, and a steering wheel! Though they had automotive elements, they were definitely trains at heart, and had even been patterned after an experimental Santa Fe prototype named the Aerotrain, in both design and function. In fact, the working title for the project had been the "Streamline Train." The two six-unit trains used were called the Tomorrowland and Fantasyland Viewliners, with names for the cars such as Jupiter, Venus, Mars, Mercury, and Saturn for the Tomorrowland Viewliner; and Alice, Bambi, Cinderella, Pinocchio, and Tinker Belle [sic] for the Fantasyland Viewliner. Perhaps in tribute to Disneyland, the Oregon Zoo maintains to this day another replica of the Aerotrain, with their version named the "Zooliner."

79. **Who was the original "sponsor" of Space Mountain?** For many years, Space Mountain was sponsored by Federal Express, though when it premiered in 1977 it was supposedly sponsored

by "DASA" —Disneyland Aeronautics and Space
Administration. There had been no actual sponsor, of course;
the play on words meant to imply NASA's involvement. NASA
did eventually sponsor an exhibit at Disneyland; in 1998, with
the new Tomorrowland, an exhibit on NASA's activities, plans,
and discoveries was opened in the former space of the Premiere
Shop.

80. <u>What radio station does Star Tours' labor-avoiding droid G29T
listen to during the Sector Two portion of the queue?</u> K-DROID
on FM 109.7, a station that he comments plays his favorite song
"I Wanna Weld Your Hand."

81. <u>Where did the Imagineers find the Calamarian for the security
booth in the overflow section of the Star Tours queue?</u> This
Calamarian comes from an often-overlooked part of the older
Star Tours queue, the control booth near the ceiling in Sector
One. Typically, Guests do not see these Audio-Animatronics
from the queue, though they are visible if you know where to
look. However, they were readily visible from the PeopleMover
track. When the Rocket Rods replaced the PeopleMover,
though, it was obvious that the vehicles did not linger in the
area long enough to appreciate the animation of the characters.
So when the Park identified the need for a longer queue area for
Star Tours and opened up the adjacent unused space, one of the
Calamarian was simply moved over into the new Security
Checkpoint. This was an example of everything falling into
place: moving the line indoors was necessary to free up space in
the New Tomorrowland, crowded by people desiring to see the
Rocket Rods (among other new attractions), and it was only
poetic justice that the Rods rendered the Calamarian in the
control booth largely unnecessary. Two Calamarian figures still
remain in the control booth.

82. <u>What did Space Station X-1 change its name to?</u> Satellite View
of America. This presentation was around at Opening Day in
1955, and offered a three-minute stylized view of America as
seen from a 500-mile-high orbit. Guests traveled from the

eastern to the western coast of America as the lighting changed, via lamps and other blacklights, from dawn to dusk. It was a doughnut-shaped building that Guests traveled through via a slow-moving sidewalk. Master matte painter Peter Ellenshaw designed and helped paint the large circular mural that Guests saw below them.

83. **Who composed the orchestral score for the queue in the Rocket Rods?** Steve Bartek, a composer and orchestrator of film soundtracks throughout the 1990s, arranged the music in the queue. He was also a member of a popular 1980s rock band in Los Angeles named Oingo Boingo. However, the music is not entirely original; Bartek arranged a new orchestration of the Sherman Brothers' song "Detroit," which was first seen in *The Happiest Millionaire*.

Fantasyland

Fantasyland Questions

Section One - Easy

1. How many lands share a border with Fantasyland?
     a. Two
     b. Three
     c. Four
     d. Five

2. What attraction concludes with a journey through Hell?
     a. Mr. Toad's Wild Ride
     b. Pinocchio's Daring Journey
     c. Peter Pan's Flight
     d. Snow White's Scary Adventures

3. What politically important country do we <u>not</u> pass through on our journey through "it's a small world"?
     a. The Netherlands
     b. China
     c. Mexico
     d. United States

4. What Fantasyland attraction featured a Swiss-type chalet?
   a. Storybook Land Canal Boats
   b. Alice in Wonderland
   c. Skyway
   d. Motorboat Cruise

5. In which attraction is Tobacco Row?
   a. Peter Pan's Flight
   b. Snow White's Scary Adventures
   c. Pinocchio's Daring Journey
   d. Mr. Toad's Wild Ride

6. What did the Pirate Ship at Skull Rock originally sell?
   a. Rock Candy
   b. Tuna fish sandwiches
   c. Grape Juice
   d. Hardtack and biscuits

7. Who watches you from above in the Castle courtyard of Fantasyland?
   a. The Evil Queen from *Snow White*
   b. Maleficent the dragon
   c. Ursula the sea witch
   d. Captain Hook

8. How many Abominable Snowmen do you see on each ride through the Matterhorn, no matter which side of the mountain you ride?

a. Two
b. Three
c. Four
d. Five

9. What phrase, often memorized by repeat visitors to Disneyland, is told to us via automated speaker as our Matterhorn bobsled approaches its unload point?
    a. "Keep your hands and arms inside at all times"
    b. "Remain seated please"
    c. "Hang on to them hats and glasses"
    d. "You are cleared for launch"

10. What was the first project done at Disneyland under the new corporate leadership of Michael Eisner and Frank Wells?
    a. Fantasyland rehab in 1983
    b. Skyway removal
    c. Mickey's Toontown
    d. Videopolis

11. What was the name of the snack stand at Videopolis?
    a. Cheetah's
    b. Meeko's
    c. Yumz
    d. Unnamed

12. When compared to the original mountain in Switzerland, what scale is the Matterhorn?
    a. 5/8th
    b. 1/8th
    c. 1/12th
    d. 1/100th

13. An orchestral version of which song plays at the Mad Tea Party?
    a. "Happy Birthday"
    b. "A Very Merry Un-Birthday (to You)"
    c. "Heffalumps and Woozles"
    d. "I'm Late (for a Very Important Date)"

14. Who was the original sponsor of the Pirate Ship?
    a. Welch's
    b. Swift
    c. Stouffer's
    d. Chicken of the Sea

15. What attraction was removed on November 9, 1994?
    a. Skyway
    b. Motorboat Cruise
    c. Fantasyland Autopia
    d. Videopolis

16. Which is <u>not</u> one of the three Fantasyland attractions that were opened with Disneyland in 1955 but later moved to a new location?

    a. King Arthur Carrousel
    b. Snow White's Scary Adventures
    c. Dumbo the Flying Elephant
    d. Mad Tea Party

17. What attraction was new to Fantasyland in 1983?

    a. Snow White's Scary Adventures
    b. Peter Pan's Flight
    c. Mr. Toad's Wild Ride
    d. Pinocchio's Daring Journey

Section Two - Medium

18. During the filming of which movie was Walt inspired to build his own Matterhorn?

    a. *The Shaggy D.A.*
    b. *Herbie the Love Bug*
    c. *The Living Desert*
    d. *Beaver Valley*
    e. *Third Man on the Mountain*
    f. *The Jungle Book*

19. What is the Motorboat Cruise loading dock now known as?
    a. Motorboat Glen
    b. Fantasia Gardens
    c. Light Magic Way
    d. Avalon Cove
    e. Romance Alley
    f. Fantasy Retreat

20. What was "Gummi Glen"?
    a. A famous Cast Member working on "it's a small world"
    b. An infamous saltwater taffy sale in Fantasyland
    c. The former name of a Fantasyland shop
    d. The leader of the Gummi Bears, invented for Disneyland
    e. A Gummi Bears' meet-and-greet area
    f. The temporary conversion of the Motorboat Cruise into a Gummi Bears theme

21. What object in Fantasyland is touch-sensitive?
    a. The Sword in the Stone
    b. Mirror in the Mad Hatter shop
    c. Monstro's teeth
    d. Snow White's Wishing Well

    e.   Brass apple at Snow White's Scary Adventures

    f.   Village Haus menu signpost

22. What does J. Thaddeus Toad's family crest say?

    a.   "Toadi Acceleratio Semper Absurda"

    b.   "Toadi Acceleratio Absurda"

    c.   "Toadi Acceleratio"

    d.   "Toadi Semper Fi"

    e.   "Toadi Gladius Dei"

    f.   "Toadi Pluribus Unum"

23. What addition almost happened to Storybook Land?

    a.   Mount Everest

    b.   Mount Olympus

    c.   Fire Mountain

    d.   Villain Mountain

    e.   Rock Candy Mountain

    f.   Witch Mountain

24. What was the original name of the Storybook Land Canal Boats?

    a.   Disney Villages

    b.   Disney Chalets

    c.   Waterways of the World

    d.   Villages of the World

    e.   Gondolas of the World

    f.   Canal Boats of the World

25. What Disney artist is responsible for the facade and look of "it's a small world"?
    a. Claude Coats
    b. Ken Anderson
    c. Peter Ellenshaw
    d. Mary Blair
    e. Hendel Butoy
    f. Marc Davis

26. What is the scale of the Storybook Land buildings?
    a. $1/100^{th}$
    b. $1/12^{th}$
    c. $1/8^{th}$
    d. $1/4^{th}$
    e. $5/8^{th}$
    f. $3/4^{th}$

27. What is not one of the names of the Mr. Toad's Wild Ride vehicles?
    a. Chelle
    b. Moley
    c. Winky
    d. Cyril
    e. Mac Badger
    f. Ratty

28. Which is not one of the names of the Storybook boats?
    a. Flower
    b. Flora

c. Fauna
d. Faline
e. Cinderella
f. Minnie

29. In what year was the Matterhorn Bobsleds'
capacity doubled?
    a. 1974
    b. 1975
    c. 1976
    d. 1977
    e. 1978
    f. 1979

30. What attraction opened later than the
other attractions in both the original and
new Fantasyland?
    a. Alice in Wonderland
    b. Dumbo the Flying Elephant
    c. King Arthur Carrousel
    d. Snow White's Scary Adventures
    e. Mr. Toad's Wild Ride

Section Three - Difficult

31. What is the area between the Matterhorn
and "it's a small world" called?

32. How was "it's a small world" inaugurated as a voyage across "Seven Seas"?

33. What Disney animated features have two attractions dedicated to them in Fantasyland?

34. What was the Matterhorn Bobsleds' claim to fame when it opened in 1959?

35. What temporary theme did the Fantasyland Autopia take on during 1991?

36. How was the Snow White attraction altered in the 1983 rehab of Fantasyland?

37. Where is the last remaining Motor Boat Cruise boat?

38. What Christmas songs are sung in "it's a small world holiday"?

39. The elephant ride was not conceived as Dumbo originally. What was it to have been?

40. What Fantasyland attraction opened two years before its film counterpart?

41. Which elements of Storybook Land do not come from feature-length Disney movies?

42. What was the difference between the Junior Autopia and the Midget Autopia?

43. Where does the money from Snow White Wishing Well go?

44. What set/scene from the Alice in Wonderland ride was removed when it was refurbished in 1983?

45. What function do the cones atop the Matterhorn serve?

46. What is the name of one of the horses on the Carrousel?

47. In what year was King Arthur Carrousel originally built?

48. What was the name of the planned traveling exhibit of miniatures that inspired Storybook Land?

49. Which is the largest building in Storybook Land?

50. What shop replaced Merlin's Magic Shop?

51. What kind of plants were chosen to line the edges of the moat at Sleeping Beauty Castle, and why?

Fantasyland
Answers

Section One - Easy

1. <u>**How many lands share a border with Fantasyland?**</u> C. Four. Fantasyland is the closest thing to the center of Disneyland, containing Sleeping Beauty Castle at one end — subsequently sharing a border with Main Street — and sharing other borders with Tomorrowland, Mickey's Toontown, and Frontierland. The three lands that have no direct contact with Fantasyland are New Orleans Square, Critter Country, and Adventureland. The Hub (a.k.a. the Central Plaza) was, incidentally, the only way to reach each land in the early days of the Park; the lands were not connected to each other in any other fashion (except for a path between Frontierland and Adventureland).

2. <u>**Which attraction concludes with a journey through Hell?**</u> A. Mr. Toad's Wild Ride. The steamy humidity of this conclusion to the ride contrasts sharply with the air-conditioned sets that preceded it and with the normally arid Californian climate outside the ride. Many glasses get fogged up by this part of the ride!

3. <u>**What politically important country do we not pass through on our journey through "it's a small world"?**</u> D. United States. Most every other major region, if not country, is represented in some manner or other, even if only by insinuation. But the United States of America does not appear, reflecting the bias that American tourists wish to see more exotic places than their own locale. The same is true for the overseas Magic Kingdoms — you will not see Japan represented in Tokyo Disneyland nor France when visiting Disneyland Paris. However, their versions of "it's

a small world" do feature a "Small World" vision of America, with the Golden Gate Bridge, Statue of Liberty, cowboys and Indians, and so on. In 1999, small painted flats of the Golden Gate Bridge and Statue of Liberty were added to the conclusion of Disneyland's version (when we pass by messages saying goodbye in various languages).

4. <u>What Fantasyland attraction featured a Swiss-type chalet?</u> C. Skyway. The Skyway to Tomorrowland was removed in 1994. The chalet remains standing, empty and unused, in the wooded area above Storybook Land and the Casey Jr. Circus Train. The theme is no accident; the Skyway technology had been bought from the Von Roll Company, a Swiss corporation, as part of the Park's first major expansion in 1956. Setting a precedent for other Disneyland attractions to come, the Skyway was the first overhead transportation system of its kind in the United States. The opening ceremony on June 23 included yodelers and dancers, as well as Dr. Walter Schmid, the Swiss Consul General in Los Angeles at the time.

5. <u>In which attraction is Tobacco Row?</u> C. Pinocchio's Daring Journey. Tobacco Row is part of the Pleasure Island sequence. Pinocchio and Lampwick, the boy who tempted Pinocchio into Pleasure Island, are transformed by their misbehavior into donkeys and then almost sold into slavery, before being swallowed by Monstro the whale.

6. <u>What did the Pirate Ship at Skull Rock originally sell?</u> B. Tuna. The official name of the location was the Chicken of the Sea Pirate Ship and Restaurant, offering Chicken of the Sea tuna fish sandwiches and assorted beverages. In keeping with the Peter Pan theme (a "Skull Rock" had already been added in the early 1960s), it was renamed Captain Hook's Galley in 1969.

7. <u>Who watches you from above in the Castle courtyard of Fantasyland?</u> A. The Evil Queen from *Snow White and the Seven Dwarfs*. She peers out every few minutes from a window above Snow White's Scary Adventures. It's one of those details

that is unheralded and thus real easy to miss — but it makes for a great discovery!

8. <u>How many Abominable Snowmen do you see on each ride through the Matterhorn, no matter which side of the mountain you ride?</u> B. Two. The first Snowman is seen by both sides of the track, then each side peels off to an individual track layout and sees an additional monster in a cave shrouded with mist. Both sides also contain a pair of red eyes and a monster's growl at the top of the lifthill, but there is no monster here to see, only to hear.

9. <u>What phrase, often repeated by repeat visitors to Disneyland, is told to us via automated speaker as our Matterhorn Bobsled approaches its unload point?</u> B. "Remain seated please. Permanecer sentados por favor." The Spanish portion of the phrase is sometimes garbled into "cinnamon toast and tacos, por favor" by non-Spanish speaking Guests. The phrase is uttered by Jack Wagner, whose voice is otherwise heard in many locations at Disneyland. Jack once related that he tried to stand up prematurely after his ride on the Matterhorn was complete, but was reminded to stay seated by his own voice!

10. <u>What was the first project done at Disneyland under the new corporate leadership of Michael Eisner and Frank Wells?</u> D. Videopolis. This new dance club, built in a meadow adjacent to "it's a small world," was billed as the "first, fastest, and finest" when it opened in 1985: the first project post-Eisner/Wells, the fastest Disneyland project ever (just 105 days from inception to reality), and the finest dance club. Of course, it did not remain a dance club, as Disneyland eventually decided that the facility was better utilized as a stage for the Park's shows.

11. <u>What was the name of the snack stand at Videopolis?</u> C. Yumz, which served pizza slices and drinks. It kept this name long after the location became a theater instead of a dance arena, with brief service as Louie's in 1991 for the "Disney Afternoon Live!" celebration. The arrival of the Pocahontas stage show in 1995

saw this facility's name changed to Meeko's, though only register receipts would acknowledge the fact. There was never a sign announcing its name after 1997, but officially its name from 1997 to 2000 was Fantasyland Theatre Snacks. Then, in 2001, it became Troubadour Treats.

12. **When compared to the original mountain in Switzerland, what scale is the Matterhorn?** B. 1/100th. The real Matterhorn, straddling the border between Switzerland and Italy in the Alps, is 14,692 feet above sea level, making Disneyland's 147 feet tall. The trees on and near the base aren't fully scaled to the mountain, of course, though smaller trees were selected to fit the illusion better. The various crags and peaks on the mountain are recreated exactly as they appear on the full-size mountain in Zermatt, Switzerland. Even the peak of the Disneyland attraction points in the same direction!

13. **An orchestral version of which song plays at the Mad Tea Party?** B. "A Very Merry Un-Birthday (to You)." Naturally, every day which is not your birthday is, by definition, your un-birthday, so most of us in fact are celebrating our un-birthday when we visit Disneyland.

14. **Who was the original sponsor of the Pirate Ship?** D. Chicken of the Sea. The Pirate Ship remained (in one form or another) at Disneyland from Opening Day until the new Fantasyland refurbishment caused it to close in August, 1982. During the course of its 27 years at Disneyland, occasionally pieces of its wood construction had to be replaced with concrete. Initial plans called for saving the Pirate Ship (by relocating it elsewhere in Fantasyland), but its condition prevented this. Even the figurehead shattered when Imagineers tried to haul it away. Some have claimed that the Pirate Ship in Disneyland Paris is the same prop, but this is an urban legend. Disneyland's version was bulldozed in 1982.

15. **What attraction was removed on November 9, 1994?** A. Skyway. Exactly five years later — right down to the date of

November 9 — the Skyway at Walt Disney World Resort's Magic Kingdom was also closed, signaling the end of sky rides at Disney theme parks in America.

16. **Which is not one of the three Fantasyland attractions that were opened with Disneyland in 1955 but later moved to a new location?** B. Snow White's Scary Adventures. King Arthur Carrousel, Dumbo the Flying Elephant, and the Mad Tea Party were all moved in the shuffle of attractions during the 1983 rehab of Fantasyland, which saw the elimination of colorful striped banners in favor of permanent, better-themed façades for the buildings, as well as more defined sets for the dark rides.

17. **What attraction was new to Fantasyland in 1983?** D. Pinocchio's Daring Journey. First debuting at Tokyo Disneyland on April 15, 1983, it opened at Disneyland with the new Fantasyland on May 25, 1983. Interestingly, that year marked the 100th anniversary of the Pinocchio story, first created in 1883 by Carlo Collodi. Pinocchio's Daring Journey occupies the former space of the Fantasyland Theatre (first known as the Mickey Mouse Club Theater). It was here that old Disney shorts were shown in an air-conditioned theater — a nice respite from a busy day at Disneyland, in a time when this was, incredibly, the only air-conditioned facility at the park. In the early days of the Mickey Mouse Club Theater, it would often show *3D Jamboree* and other special 3D footage of the Mouseketeers. The name "Fantasyland Theatre" would reappear as that of the renovated Videopolis when it was reopened as a stage-show venue in 1995.

Section Two - Medium

18. **During the filming of which movie was Walt inspired to build his own Matterhorn?** E. *Third Man on the Mountain*. Walt was frequently inspired to create attractions based on films he was working on — one need only look to the rest of Fantasyland for

examples of this — but the Matterhorn was also born out of a desire to invigorate that area of Fantasyland. In 1959, a huge development project was undertaken that involved putting in the Submarine Voyage and landscaping the roof to allow for the two Autopias and the Disneyland-Alweg monorail system. The Matterhorn was also constructed at this time, becoming one of the first major expansions for the Park.

19. **What is the Motorboat Cruise loading dock now known as?** B. Fantasia Gardens. The area is not used in any sense of the word, and in fact remains one of the few tranquil locations in the Park. A small waterfall bubbles nearby; this is the source of the water for the lagoon, which drains downhill all across Fantasyland, Adventureland, and Frontierland, so that the areas with "dark water" (such as the Jungle Cruise and the Rivers of America) all share the same water, before it gets pumped back up to Storybook Land and the Motorboat Lagoon.

20. **What was "Gummi Glen?"** F. The temporary conversion of the Motorboat Cruise into a Gummi Bears theme. This temporary theme happened during the "Disney Afternoon Live!" celebration at Disneyland in 1991. Much like the Fantasyland Autopia's conversion, the Motorboat Cruise was converted to the Gummi Bears, featuring large colorful cutouts of the characters from the show. It added a bit of atmosphere to a ride that was otherwise interesting only in its relaxation factor, but did little more than advertise the show.

21. **What object in Fantasyland is touch-sensitive?** E. Brass apple at Snow White's Scary Adventures. It's not the Sword in the Stone, as you might expect (that is released via remote control during the ceremony), but rather the apple above the open book at the start of the Snow White queue. If you touch the apple, you will hear the Evil Queen cackle. Few Guests even know it's there. Vexingly, the apple is high enough that children – the very segment of the public most likely to touch everything – aren't often able to reach it.

22. **What does J. Thaddeus Toad's family crest say?** A. "Toadi Acceleratio Semper Absurda." Translated into English, this means "speeding with Toad is always absurd." It is, of course, Toad's obsession with speed which forms the basis for *Wind in the Willows* as well as the Disneyland attraction. This phrase also provides the inspiration for the subtitle for this book.

23. **What addition almost happened to Storybook Land?** E. Rock Candy Mountain. There were plans for an addition to the Storybook area called "Rock Candy Mountain" that would be populated inside by figures from the Disney movie *Rainbow Road to Oz*, a story the Disney Studios had recently bought the options on. However, the model for the exterior of Rock Candy Mountain was built from real lollipops and candy, and it became a sticky unappealing mess, so it was abandoned. The Oz universe would not resurface in Disneyland, though some miniature figures of characters for the model still reside at the Walt Disney Archives. There is an Oz connection, however, in two other Disney attractions: The Great Movie Ride at Disney-MGM Studios in Walt Disney World Resort and Le Pays des Contes de Fées (Storybook Land Canal Boats) at Disneyland Paris Park. In Paris' Storybook attraction, the final miniature model seen at the attraction is a wonderful Emerald City (prompting many visitors to wonder what this apparently non-Disney reference is doing in Disneyland Paris; the answer is that Disney made the movie *Return to Oz*).

24. **What was the original name of the Storybook Land Canal Boats?** F. Canal Boats of the World. However, employees quickly dubbed it the "Mud Bank Ride." There was nothing to look at! The miniatures had not been built for the ride, nor were there nicely landscaped flowers on the hills; there were quite simply mud banks. The ostensible theme that first summer was that these were canal boats, cruising through urban canals such as one can find in Venice or Amsterdam, but more honestly the ride had simply been a victim to budgetary and time constraints shortly before Park opening. This was the first Disneyland attraction closed, open just two months before ceasing operation

on September 16, 1955. As quickly as he could, Walt revived his original idea for a Lilliputian Land and reworked it into miniature villages re-enacting scenes from classic Disney films, thereby creating today's Storybook Land.

25. **What Disney artist is responsible for the façade and look of "it's a small world"?** D. Mary Blair. Mary was one of several Disney employees to go on a trip to Latin America in 1941 that resulted in *Saludos Amigos* and *The Three Caballeros*. Eventually she moved over to WED and designed tile murals for Walt Disney World Resort's Contemporary Resort and for the new Tomorrowland in 1967. Her work on "it's a small world" included a white façade with gold accents, which was altered in later years to a conglomeration of multicolored pastels. In 2002, Disneyland repainted the façade back to the original white with gold accents.

26. **What is the scale of the Storybook Land buildings?** B. 1/12th. Working with such a scale made it much easier to convert heights and lengths; instead of feet, cottages and castles could be built an equivalent number of inches high. This is of course a much smaller scale than is used elsewhere (such as the sternwheeler or the railroads), but that is part of the charm of the miniature villages. The miniature trees came from a pygmy forest near Mendocino in northern California, where the pines grew to just 3 to 12 feet. The pygmy forest's conditions arise from soil with low nutrients and high acidity, and roots cannot penetrate the clay a few feet below the ground. As a result, the growth of the forest is quite stunted. Many of the trees in Storybook grow no more than one inch per year.

27. **What is not one of the names of the Mr. Toad's Wild Ride vehicles?** A. Chelle. The correct names are Toady, Ratty, Weasel, Mac Badger, Moley, Winky and Cyril, all of which are names of characters from *The Wind in the Willows*. Mr. Toad is also represented in the Storybook Land Canal Boats; his Toad Manor once stood where Agrabah now resides, and the manor was temporarily removed until it found a new home near the

miniature windmills. The Toad Manor is even capable of producing smoke out of its many chimneys!

28. <u>Which is not one of the names of the Storybook boats?</u> F. Minnie. In the days of the Canal Boats of the World, the boats were called Katrina, Lady Katrina, Wendy, Lady of Shallot, Aurora, Nellie Bly, Gretel, Annie Oakley, Bold Lochinvar, Cinderella, Lady Guenivere [sic], and Lady of the Lake. When it became Storybook, the boats were renamed Cinderella, Daisy, Aurora, Alice, Faline, Flora, Fauna, Flower, Katrina, Merryweather, Wendy, Snow White, and Tinker Bell. In the 1990s, Belle and Ariel replaced Gretel and Katrina, which had survived as boat names beyond the original Storybook conversion.

29. <u>In what year was the Matterhorn Bobsleds' capacity doubled?</u> E. 1978. While the Matterhorn has always had two sides, the attraction's capacity was hampered by the low number of riders per bobsled. In 1978, with the addition of tandem bobsleds and a computer-controlled ride system, the attraction was able to funnel through more people per hour. This complete refurbishment also saw the addition of the famed Abominable Snowman.

30. <u>What attraction opened later than the other attractions in both the original and new Fantasyland?</u> A. Alice in Wonderland. True to form, the attraction was "late for a very important date." It didn't open until nearly three years after the other Fantasyland dark rides, making its debut on June 14, 1958, the same day as the Sailing Ship Columbia on the Rivers of America. It was also late in opening after the major renovation it received with the rest of Fantasyland, though for a good reason — at Disney, quality is always preferred over speed. There simply weren't enough resources to get the work done.

Section Three - Difficult

31. <u>What is the area between the Matterhorn and "it's a small world" called?</u> Small World Way. Also known as the Small World Mall and the Small World Promenade, this zone served as the home of "Disney Afternoon Avenue," and provided much space for temporary exhibits and booths throughout the Park promotions of the late 1980s including a beach scene for "Blast to the Past" and Midway Games for "State Fair." In 1997 it was remodeled into a prime parade viewing area specifically for the nighttime "streetacular" Light Magic, and outfitted with light towers and a pedestrian bypass of the parade route, providing a quick way to get to Mickey's Toontown even when the production was underway.

32. <u>How was "it's a small world" inaugurated as a voyage across "Seven Seas"?</u> The attraction depicts a journey across all the continents — well, except Antarctica — so the slogan refers to the earth's seven oceans and implies that we travel around the world. To commemorate the fact, and perhaps to lend credibility to the claim, Walt Disney inaugurated "it's a small world" by dropping in water samples from each of the world's seven oceans.

33. <u>What Disney animated features have two attractions dedicated to them in Fantasyland?</u> *Alice in Wonderland* and *Dumbo. Alice* is represented by the Alice in Wonderland dark ride and the Mad Tea Party (not to mention the shop the Mad Hatter), while *Dumbo* has both the Flying Elephants and the Casey Jr. Circus Train. *Sleeping Beauty* had the Castle — with its charming walk-through attraction — as well as the Carrousel (until 2002, when the panels were removed). The carrousel is named after a character from *The Sword in the Stone* — King Arthur — but its panels display scenes from *Sleeping Beauty*, so it could arguably have been considered an attraction dedicated to either movie (the panels were added in 1975, when the horses were repainted from many colors to all be white). The mismatching

of attractions seems to be a theme in Fantasyland; at Walt Disney World Resort, for years the fine dining restaurant in Cinderella Castle was named King Stefan's Banquet Hall, even though King Stefan is Sleeping Beauty's father, not Cinderella's! This was finally remedied in the late 1990s when the restaurant was renamed Cinderella's Royal Table. For a time, *Peter Pan* also had its fair share of representation, though not all in the form of attractions. Before the removal of the Pirate Ship and Skull Rock in 1982, *Peter Pan* was represented in the form of the above mentioned restaurant, Peter Pan Flight, and Tinker Bell's Toy Shoppe.

34. **What was the Matterhorn Bobsleds' claim to fame when it opened in 1959?** It was the world's first tubular steel coaster. Steel coasters had existed before, but they had flat steel tracks rather than a tube, as most all steel coasters have today. Oddly, the Matterhorn was listed as a Tomorrowland attraction when it opened, and was only later "moved" to Fantasyland (merely by relabeling its location on park maps). Though not particularly futuristic in theme, the Matterhorn debuted with the Submarine Voyage and the monorail, and so it was simplest to label the expansion as a Tomorrowland upgrade.

35. **What temporary theme did the Fantasyland Autopia take on during 1991?** Chip and Dale's Rescue Rangers. "Disney Afternoon Live!," which was concentrated on Small World Way and the back areas of Fantasyland, was one of the big Parkwide promotions of the time period. Cardboard cutouts were placed throughout the Fantasyland Autopia track, and the attraction was renamed Rescue Rangers Raceway, while the Tomorrowland Autopia remained unchanged. It did little to add atmosphere and instead worked more like an advertisement for the Disney animation programming.

36. **How was the Snow White attraction altered in the 1983 rehab of Fantasyland?** The figure of Snow White herself was added to the ride, in the dwarfs' cottage. The ride was also made more frightening with extended dungeon scenes. In addition to this,

the ride's capacity was doubled with the addition of a second row to the ride vehicles.

37. **Where is the last remaining Motor Boat Cruise boat?** When the ride was removed in 1993, the boats were simply put into storage in the warehouses behind Disneyland, and the loading dock was converted into a relaxing place to sit. One of the boats was integrated into the design of the employee cafeteria "The Eat Ticket" (get it?) near the new administration building, along with one of the Skyway buckets, Dumbo elephants, and Autopia and PeopleMover cars. All now hang from the ceiling over the heads of the eating Cast Members.

38. **What Christmas songs are sung in "it's a small world holiday"?** The theme song "It's a Small World (After All)" is still represented, but it alternates with "Jingle Bells" throughout the ride. Resultantly, because the tones and rhythms vary under this scenario, the ride feels less repetitive to many visitors. The finale of the ride has been set off to different music, namely "Deck the Halls," so it was necessary to create a zone of quiet to insure that the songs would not overlap in a cacophony. To achieve this quiet zone, the final rainforest section is draped over and silent, with tinsel setting the scene. Combined with the stunningly gorgeous nighttime exterior lights and the redecorating that occurs within the ride, the songs transform "it's a small world" into a must-see E-Ticket attraction all over again, fully armed with the kind of charm that characterized its beginnings in 1964. You can also briefly hear "Afi Shia Pa" in the African section of the ride, and "Feliz Navidad" in Latin America.

39. **The elephant ride was not conceived as Dumbo originally. What was it to have been?** "Pink Elephants on Parade." The original idea of the ride was that the Guest would be surrounded by the pink elephants just as Dumbo was when drunk; like the dark rides, the Guest was cast in the role of the main character rather than seeing him/her. However, Walt changed his mind about the pink elephants because he was concerned that the ride

might send the wrong message to children about alcohol. The band organ next to Dumbo came to Disneyland from Italy — made in 1915 by Gavioli — for intended installation in Bear Country, but was not used until the 1983 refurbishment of Fantasyland.

40. **What Fantasyland attraction opened two years before its film counterpart?** Sleeping Beauty Castle Walk-Thru. The dioramas first appeared in the Castle in 1957, two years before the movie premiered. Similar 3D scenes have also long been a staple in the Emporium for each new animated movie release.

41. **Which elements of Storybook Land do not come from feature-length Disney movies?** There are sets based on *Lullaby Land* and *The Old Mill* (two Silly Symphonies), and the houses of the pigs from the *Three Little Pigs*. There is also a set based on *Wind in the Willows*, but strictly speaking it is a portion of a full-length feature, *The Adventures of Ichabod and Mr. Toad*.

42. **What was the difference between the Junior Autopia and the Midget Autopia?** The Tomorrowland Autopia came first, opening with the Park in 1955. When that proved extremely popular, the Junior Autopia was opened on the site of the failed Mickey Mouse Club Circus. However, the smaller (and simpler track layout) didn't provide much of a solution to the demand for more Autopia capacity. In 1959, the Fantasyland Autopia was constructed on the site of the closed Junior Autopia. But the kids did get another Autopia all their own — the Midget Autopia. This attraction, located where "it's a small world" now is, featured cars tailored to young drivers…in fact, adults weren't even allowed on the attraction! When "the Happiest Cruise that Ever Sailed" came to Disneyland, the Midget Autopia had to be removed.

43. **Where does the money from Snow White Wishing Well go?** Children's charities. Originally, it was put into a trust established between Disneyland and the Variety Clubs International, to go to such places as orphanages, schools and

children's homes. The trust was terminated in 1972 when federal regulations restricted contributions to foreign charities, and now it goes to domestic children's charities.

44. <u>What set/scene from the Alice in Wonderland ride was removed when it was refurbished in 1983?</u> The upside-down room was replaced by a woods scene with Tweedledee and Tweedledum. Additionally, the Oversized Room (which symbolized Alice shrinking) was incorporated into the singing flowers room, as the vehicles ascend to the second story in the building. Alice in Wonderland shares a building with the Mr. Toad attraction, so Alice has to rise above Toad to find enough space for the attraction. The finale of the ride, added by Imagineer Tony Baxter, travels through the former machine shop (and rehab center) for the ride's vehicles. The remodeling of the attraction saw Kathryn Beaumont, the original voice of Alice from the 1951 movie, return to record new voice samples, as well as the addition of new incidental ride music created by Kathryn and John Debney.

45. <u>What function do the cones atop the Matterhorn serve?</u> The tall cone is an airplane beacon, which is illuminated to inform low-flying planes that the otherwise unlit structure is there and presents a possible hazard. There is also a lightning rod atop the Matterhorn, designed to lure lightning away from the ground, people, or otherwise sensitive electronic equipment throughout the Park. In 1961 a bright Christmas star, installed by Santa, was placed atop the Matterhorn, where it remained during holiday seasons until the energy crisis of the 1970s.

46. <u>What is the name of one of the horses on the Carrousel?</u> Until the 2002-2003 refurbishment which added a bench, there were seventy-two horses on the carrousel. Not all the horses are doing the same thing; some may be leaping, cantering, galloping, or simply standing. Most of them have names: Alma, Arabian Knight, Avanti, Aztec, Baby, Bink, Blue, Brandy, Bruce, Centurion, Champion, Checkers Jr., Cinch, Copper, Crown Jewel, Crusader, Dagger, Daisy, Dante, Doubloon, Duke, Eagle

Scout, Elroy, Emerald, Fern, Galaxy, Gigalo, Gypsy, Ivy, Jester, Jingles (who has a Hidden Mickey in the form of three jewels arranged in a familiar pattern, and was the "lead horse" used when counting rotations of the turntable, before the process became automated), Keiffer, King Richard, Lance, Lucifer's Rose, Marilyn, Melissa, National Velvet, Nipper, Patches, Penny, Queenie, Rally, Red Devil, Renaissance, Sapphire, Saxon, Sea Biscuit, St. Patrick, Streamer, Tartan, Tassel, Testy Pat, Tiny, Topaz, Tulip, Unice, and Valance.

47. **In what year was King Arthur Carrousel originally built?** 1875. It was built by hand in Toronto, Canada, and it is a Dentzel model, referring to Gustav Dentzel, who built carrousels full-time from a company in Philadelphia.

48. **What was the name of the planned traveling exhibit of miniatures that inspired Storybook Land?** "Disneylandia." While the idea of Disneyland was still germinating in his brain, Walt pulled a few employees from the Disney Studios (including Roger Broggie, Wathel Rogers, and Ken Anderson) to work on miniature dancing figures — a very primitive form of Audio-Animatronics, a term that Walt himself would later coin, as a mixture of animation and electronics (the audio component referred to a process of controlling electronics via audio impulses on an optical strip of film).

49. **Which is the largest building in Storybook Land?** Cinderella's Chateau, which was completely replaced in 1988 due to its constant exposure to the sun and the elements. It is composed, like most miniatures in Storybook, of a wooden framework soaked with resin, with fiberglass panels on the exterior cast from sculpted wooden molds.

50. **What shop replaced Merlin's Magic Shop?** Mickey's Christmas Chalet. Merlin's Magic Shop was one of the opening day shops in the Park, located centrally in the Sleeping Beauty Castle courtyard. In 1983, with the complete overhaul of Fantasyland, the shop changed to Mickey's Christmas Chalet, featuring

Christmas decorations and the holiday mood year-round. One of the most popular shops to grace this location was the Villains Shop, which was located here from 1991 to 1996 and again, to the relief of collectors of villains merchandise, from 1998 to 2002 (under the name "Villains Lair").

51. **What kind of plants were chosen to line the edges of the moat at Sleeping Beauty Castle, and why?** Junipers were chosen to provide most of the vegetation because the swans — which are certainly real — would eat most any other type of foliage. The swans are always leased by the Park, so that there is always exactly one male-female pair swimming in the moat (whose official name, seldom used, is Lake of the Swans). The original swans — both of them black and white — were a gift from the Hollywood Turf Club.

Mickey's Toontown

Mickey's Toontown Questions

Section One - Easy

1. The Bounce House is themed after which classic character?
    a. Mickey
    b. Donald
    c. Goofy
    d. Pluto

2. Which is not one of the three "zones" in Toontown?
    a. Toontown Suburbs
    b. Toontown Square
    c. Downtown Toontown
    d. Mickey's Neighborhood

3. What attraction opened later than the rest of Toontown?
    a. Gadget's Go Coaster
    b. Mickey's House
    c. Jolly Trolley
    d. Roger Rabbit's Car Toon Spin

4. What's the official name of the Toontown trolley?
    a. Toontown Trolley
    b. Mickey's Trolley
    c. Bouncing Trolley
    d. Jolly Trolley

Section Two - Medium

5. In Toontown-speak, what does "DAR" stand for?
    a. Dragons and Reptiles
    b. Drugs and Rehab
    c. Daughters of the Animated Realm
    d. Disney's Animated Realm
    e. Daughters of the Animated Reel
    f. Disney's Animated Reel

6. Which of the "Fab Five" has no house you can enter?
    a. Goofy
    b. Mickey
    c. Minnie
    d. Donald
    e. Pluto

7. What merchandise location has been added to Toontown since its opening in early 1993?
   - a. Gag Factory
   - b. Toon-Up Treats
   - c. Toontown Five & Dime
   - d. Toontown Emporium
   - e. Roger Rabbit's Replicas
   - f. Toontown Gifts

8. What was the theme to the Toontown ball crawl?
   - a. Mickey's racquetballs
   - b. Pluto's chew toys
   - c. Chip and Dale's acorns
   - d. Daisy's popcorn
   - e. Donald's golf balls
   - f. Goofy's tennis balls

9. What movie inspired Mickey's Toontown?
   - a. *Who Discovered Roger Rabbit*
   - b. *Who Killed Roger Rabbit*
   - c. *Who Framed Roger Rabbit*
   - d. *Mary Poppins*
   - e. *Song of the South*
   - f. *The Black Cauldron*

10. What is the industry term for the type of ride that Roger Rabbit's Car Toon Spin is?
    - a. Black ride
    - b. Slow ride
    - c. Tunnel of love

d. Dark ride

e. Animated ride

f. Fantasy ride

11. Mickey's Toontown was inspired by an area of Walt Disney World Resort's Magic Kingdom that similarly honored the cartoon heroes. What was its original name?

a. Toon Magic

b. Toon Lake

c. Toonville

d. Duckburg, USA

e. Mickey's Land

f. Mickey's Birthdayland

Section Three - Difficult

12. What cartoon shorts show in Mickey's Barn?

13. How does Mickey's Toontown follow a tradition of paying tribute to individuals as found on Main Street?

14. What is the name of the show that performs whenever the clock strikes a new hour?

15. In film, where did the Imagineers find a model for Mickey's house?

16. In the queue for Roger Rabbit's Car Toon Spin, several humorous license plates identify Disney characters or taglines — some old and some new. Which of these refers to the oldest Disney animation?

Mickey's Toontown
Answers

Section One - Easy

1. <u>The Bounce House is themed after which classic character?</u> C. Goofy. Evidence of his residence can be found in both the garden (the Goofy scarecrow and his outline in the pavement next to an inflatable pool he was trying to jump into are examples) as well as in the look of the house. The actual bouncing takes place in Goofy's living room, but it's only for children — this is one Disneyland attraction that Guests <u>over</u> a certain height aren't let into. Parents can, however, watch their kids jumping around on the inflatable furniture by way of a viewing area.

2. <u>Which is not one of the three "zones" in Toontown?</u> A. Toontown Suburbs. Downtown, Toontown Square, and Mickey's Neighborhood are all actual zones that make up the land. The Downtown area houses Roger Rabbit's Car Toon Spin and most of the interactive games for the children, Toontown Square in the middle contains the bandstand and the eateries, and Mickey's Neighborhood is obviously the home of the characters. Both the Downtown and residential areas feature fountains: there is one of Mickey near his house and one of Roger near his attraction.

3. <u>What attraction opened later than the rest of Toontown?</u> D. Roger Rabbit's Car Toon Spin. This ride opened in January 1994 — a full year after the debut of Toontown. It was budgeted that way; the idea was to get Mickey's Toontown open and introduced to families first, and then introduce its big attraction.

One of the primary motivating factors for building Mickey's Toontown at all was to provide a place where all Guests could reliably locate Mickey Mouse and have their picture taken with him; this would be accomplished with the inclusion of Mickey's House and thus there was some urgency to get this part of Toontown open first. Prior to 1993, one of the biggest complaints was that Mickey was not always around to greet children at the usual character spots, and Guests wanted a place to find him reliably.

4. <u>What's the official name of the Toontown trolley?</u> D. The Jolly Trolley. This Trolley is actually a fairly sophisticated device, employing the same pistons used in flight simulators in a rolling pattern. There are two trolleys, but Disneyland no longer uses both, as such a practice confuses the Guests and makes for too many hazards in the area most populated by small children. In 2001, the second trolley was auctioned off on eBay.com (a ploy also attempted unsuccessfully for the keel boats a year later).

Section Two - Medium

5. <u>In Toontown-speak, what does "DAR" stand for?</u> E. "Daughters of the Animated Reel." The entrance to Toontown dips beneath the railroad berm, allowing for the placement of a large welcome sign and several smaller, humorous signs. These include the Daughters of the Animated Reel, the Loyal Knights of the Inkwell, Optimist Intoonational, and the Benevolent and Protective Order of the Mouse.

6. <u>Which of the "Fab Five" has no house you can enter?</u> E. Pluto. He does have a doghouse next to Mickey's House, but it's nothing human-sized. His domicile is not to be confused with the counter-service food location in Mickey's Toontown by the same name; Pluto's Dog House serves hot dogs and drinks — though it's a walk-up stand and you still cannot enter it!

7. **What merchandise location has been added to Toontown since its opening in early 1993?** B. Toon-Up Treats. In December 1997, the candy store opened at the Toontown Gas Station. It remained closed most of the time, however, and became a food facility on July 19, 2002.

8. **What was the theme to the Toontown ball crawl?** C. Chip and Dale's Acorn Crawl. This attraction reproduced the popular children's play area, which made its first appearance in family eateries in the 1970s. Within a few years, however, Disneyland recognized the problems of such a play area: any child who wets himself/herself would cause the area to be closed for a thorough cleaning, and if any item were lost it would have to be closed down to track down the article.

9. **What movie inspired Mickey's Toontown?** C. *Who Framed Roger Rabbit*. The 1988 film was a joint effort between Disney and Amblin Entertainment, which utilized several non-Disney characters — Bugs Bunny and Mickey Mouse could finally face off, as could Daffy and Donald Duck.

10. **What is the industry term for the type of ride that Roger Rabbit's Car Toon Spin is?** D. Dark ride. However, this is a dark ride with a few extra twists to it. A dark ride is so named because of its reliance on "black lights," the purplish bulbs which make florescent paint glow in the dark (this makes dark rides the ideal places to check the handstamp you received at Main Gate and see if you can read it). Dark rides have been around for decades, but most do not feature fully rounded figures like Disney's, let alone animation. Though the animation is crude, Guests move past the scenery so quickly that it hardly needs to be smoother. Roger Rabbit's Car Toon Spin is different still in that it offers Guests the opportunity to control their view, or to spin crazily through the entire ride, though this gets tiring rather quickly. To test whether such a revolving vehicle could be mounted on a dark ride track, Imagineers actually

hooked up one of the Mad Tea Party Teacups on Pinocchio's Daring Journey, and it worked!

11. <u>Mickey's Toontown was inspired by an area of Walt Disney World Resort's Magic Kingdom that similarly honored the cartoon heroes. What was its original name?</u> F. Mickey's Birthdayland. It was created on the occasion of Mickey's 60th Birthday in 1988 and renamed Mickey's Starland in 1990, retained because of its popularity. Briefly rechristened Mickey's Toyland for Christmas 1995, it finally became Mickey's Toontown Fair. Disneyland's Mickey's Toontown avoided the carnivalesque tented houses of Mickey's Birthdayland, however, instead getting dedicated buildings for the interiors.

Section Three - Difficult

12. <u>What cartoon shorts show in Mickey's Barn?</u> The loop that plays in Mickey's Barn includes "trailers" for "Thru the Mirror," "The Sorcerer's Apprentice," "Steamboat Willie," and "The Band Concert," and uses various clips from assorted cartoons for filler.

13. <u>How does Mickey's Toontown follow a tradition of paying tribute to individuals as found on Main Street?</u> The second-story windows of Mickey's Toontown give credit to those who helped create it, though they are often whimsical rather than respectful.

14. <u>What is the name of the show that performs whenever the clock strikes a new hour?</u> The Clockenspiel, a play on words from the famous Glockenspiels from Germany (most notably in Munich). More directly, it reproduces the Glockenspiel that occurs every fifteen minutes at "it's a small world."

15. <u>In film, where did the Imagineers find a model for Mickey's house?</u> Nowhere! They searched through all the old Mickey

Mouse shorts and discovered, to their surprise, that Mickey's house had never been shown in its entirety. They therefore felt free to create his home from scratch, using the design from Mickey's Birthdayland as a starting place. In Mickey's Birthdayland, Disney artist Russell Schroeder used standard architects' plans and made cartoon versions of them to match the look in Disney comic books. The one rule for all of Mickey's Toontown: no straight lines! All the architecture in the land is designed to be curvy and rounded; both cartoony and non-threatening, like Mickey's features themselves.

16. **In the queue for Roger Rabbit's Car Toon Spin, several humorous license plates identify Disney characters or taglines — some old and some new. Which of these refers to the oldest Disney animation?** "3 LIL PIGS," which of course refers to the Depression-era Disney featurette *Three Little Pigs*. The plate "BB WOLF" could also be the correct answer, as it refers to the Big Bad Wolf in the same cartoon. The others on the wall are "2N TOWN" (Toontown), "MR TOAD," "1DRLND" (Wonderland), "1D N PTR" (Wendy & Peter Pan), "IM L8" (I'm late!), "CAP 10 HK" (Captain Hook), "L MERM8" (Little Mermaid), "101 DLMN" (*101 Dalmatians*), "FAN T C" (Fantasy), "RS2CAT" (*Aristocats*), and "ZPD2DA" (Zip-A-Dee-Doo-Dah).

Frontierland

Frontierland Questions

Section One - Easy

1. What is the name of the fort on Tom Sawyer Island?
    a. Fort Sawyer
    b. Fort Pioneer
    c. Fort Disney
    d. Fort Wilderness

2. What company sponsors the Conestoga Fries wagon?
    a. McDonald's
    b. Burger King
    c. Wendy's
    d. Ore-Ida

3. What happens "when the night ignites"?
    a. Fireworks begin
    b. Fantasmic! begins
    c. Streetlights turn on
    d. Staged Cowboy/Indian shootouts begin

4. Which craft on the Rivers of America was added the most recently?
   a. Mike Fink Keel Boats
   b. Canoes
   c. Mark Twain Riverboat
   d. Sailing Ship Columbia

5. Frontierland was home to Disneyland's most stubborn working animals. Which?
   a. Clydesdale horses
   b. Pack mules
   c. Indian dogs
   d. Arabian horses

6. Which is not one of the names of the rafts that transport Guests to Tom Sawyer Island?
   a. Becky Thatcher
   b. Huck Finn
   c. Mark Twain
   d. Injun Joe

7. What was the petting zoo at Disneyland called?
   a. Big Thunder Ranch
   b. Frontierland Ranch
   c. Disneyland Ranch
   d. Cascade Ranch

8. The Sailing Ship Columbia is named after which famous ship?
    a. First American ship to sail around the world
    b. First American ship to sail to China
    c. First American ship to sail around the Arctic Circle
    d. First American ship to sail across the Atlantic

9. What Davy Crockett episode was responsible for the Keel Boat attraction at Disneyland?
    a. *Davy Crockett — Indian Fighter*
    b. *Davy Crockett and the Smugglers*
    c. *Davy Crockett's Keelboat Race*
    d. *Davy Crockett's Big Competition*

10. Which was not one of the four sections of Nature's Wonderland?
    a. Rainbow Caverns
    b. Beaver Valley
    c. Living Desert
    d. Cactus Alley

11. Where was the Frito Kid located?
    a. Casa de Fritos
    b. Cabana de Fritos

    c. Pendleton shop

    d. Silver Spur shop

12. Which is not one of the names of the landings on Tom Sawyer Island?
    a. Settler's Landing
    b. Becky's Landing
    c. Tom's Landing
    d. Huck's Landing

Section Two - Medium

13. What national park served as the inspiration for Big Thunder Mountain Railroad's towering buttes?
    a. Zion
    b. Bryce Canyon
    c. Arches
    d. Death Valley
    e. Yosemite
    f. Yellowstone

14. What was the original name of the canoe attraction?
    a. Davy Crockett Canoes
    b. Davy Crockett Explorer Canoes
    c. Davy Crockett War Canoes
    d. Indian Canoes

e. Indian Explorer Canoes

f. Indian War Canoes

15. Where was Mineral Hall located?
   a. Inside Fort Wilderness
   b. At the Conestoga Wagons
   c. Next to the Golden Horseshoe
   d. Big Thunder Ranch
   e. At the Wax Museum
   f. Next to Casa de Fritos

16. At one time, Pepsi-Cola sponsored a restaurant in Disneyland. What location did they sponsor?
   a. Golden Horseshoe
   b. Casa Mexicana
   c. Aunt Jemima's Kitchen
   d. Don DeFore's Silver Banjo
   e. Stage Door Café
   f. Conestoga Fries

17. During the run of the "Festival of Fools," what name did the Big Thunder Barbecue take on?
   a. Festival of Fools Barbecue
   b. Hunchback Barbecue
   c. Festival Barbecue
   d. Festival of Foods
   e. Festival of Fools Foods
   f. Festival of Barbecue

18. What was the name of the peak along the Rivers of America?
    a. Big Thunder Peak
    b. Cascade Peak
    c. Rainbow Mountain
    d. Frontierland Peak
    e. Disney Peak
    f. Schweitzer Peak

19. What was the former name of the River Belle Terrace?
    a. Aunt Jemima's Terrace
    b. Aunt Jemima's River Belle Terrace
    c. Aunt Jemima's Breakfast House
    d. Aunt Jemima's Orleans House
    e. Aunt Jemima's Pancake House
    f. Aunt Jemima's Bed & Breakfast

20. What is the name of the path behind Big Thunder Mountain Railroad toward Fantasyland?
    a. Big Thunder Path
    b. Big Thunder Way
    c. Big Thunder Alley
    d. Big Thunder Trail
    e. Big Thunder Road
    f. Big Thunder Concourse

21. How many attractions in Frontierland were part of Opening Day and continue operating today?
   a. One
   b. Two
   c. Three
   d. Four
   e. Five
   f. Six

Section Three - Difficult

22. Why is Big Thunder Mountain so named?

23. What is the name of the project originally slated to connect Frontierland with Fantasyland and also mesh with the theming of Big Thunder Mountain Railroad?

24. Who christened the Mark Twain Riverboat?

25. What two rides predated Big Thunder Mountain Railroad on this same plot of land?

26. Who was Mickey Moo?

27. Where is the Big Thunder Mountain Railroad computer room?

28. The real stables at Disneyland are located behind the former home of Big Thunder Ranch. What is the name of this facility?

29. Where was the hull of the Mark Twain Riverboat built?

30. Who provided the narration for the Mine Train Through Nature's Wonderland attraction?

31. What 8 flags fly over the Riverboat Dock?

32. What is the target year for Frontierland's theme?

33. What are the names of the Big Thunder Mountain Railroad trains?

Frontierland
Answers

Section One - Easy

1. <u>What is the name of the fort on Tom Sawyer Island?</u> D. Fort Wilderness. This section of Frontierland was conceived as a venue for battles between Indians and white settlers, giving rise to the need for a fort of wooden logs, and accounting for the former swivel guns in the fort's towers. Fort Wilderness is also the name of the RV Campground Resort at Walt Disney World Resort.

2. <u>What company sponsors the Conestoga Fries wagon?</u> A. McDonald's. The familiar "Golden Arches" logo was visible on the special cartons for the fries when the location opened. The wagon itself has "Westward Ho" displayed across its canvas, a nod to the Disney film with the same title. Incidentally, Westward Ho was already the name of a location at Disneyland when the wagon opened in 1998; a merchandise shop at the entrance to Frontierland had had that name since 1987.

3. <u>What happens "when the night ignites"?</u> B. Fantasmic! begins. This was the tagline for Fantasmic!, the fireworks and stage show spectacular which occurs selected nights on the Rivers of America. Merchandise for the popular show, particularly in its early years, urged Guests to "be there when the night ignites!" recalling the magic of a show that emerges in all its complexity during the night but which manages to stay completely invisible during the day. Fantasmic! debuted on May 13, 1992.

4. Which craft on the Rivers of America was added the most recently? D. Sailing Ship Columbia. Walt proudly sat one day watching the busy river, already crowded with the keel boats, canoes, rafts, and the paddlewheeler, and proclaimed the need for another big boat!

5. Frontierland was home to Disneyland's most stubborn working animals. Which? B. Pack Mules. These "mules" were in fact Sardinian donkeys. The animals, all strung together, would move literally as a pack — if one stopped, then they all did. They were cheap to purchase and maintain, but the problems continued to pile up (i.e., animals eating Guests' clothing and hair, the problematic 190-pound weight limit, among others), and finally the ride, despite its popularity, was closed 3 years sooner than the Mine Train Through Nature's Wonderland.

6. Which is not one of the names of the rafts that transport Guests to Tom Sawyer Island? C. Mark Twain. Tom Sawyer, Becky Thatcher, Huck Finn and Injun Joe are all rafts that transport Guests to the island. Since 1956, the rafts have departed the Frontierland mainland from several different places, including from the Indian Village, the Frontierland Bridge (approximately where the Pirates of the Caribbean entrance is now) and its current location near Fowler's Harbor.

7. What was the petting zoo at Disneyland called? A. Big Thunder Ranch. In the center of the Ranch area was a cabin, which you could visit to see the typical dwelling of a frontier settler. Big Thunder Barbecue on the east side featured a large barn, which served as the kitchen, and the west side of the ranch was a series of stables and a souvenir store. The entire northern half of the ranch was taken up by the petting zoo itself. The entire Ranch area was the headquarters of "Santa's Workshop" during the holiday season in the late 1980s and early 1990s, but everything except the Barbecue was removed in 1996 for the Hunchback Festival Arena and stage. In 2000, even the Barbecue was closed to make way for more expansion, and its menu was folded into the revised Casa Mexicana.

8. **The Sailing Ship Columbia is named after which famous ship?**
A. First American ship to sail around the world. With its three masts, ten gunports, and 84-foot height, the Disneyland ship is a full-scale replica of the ship which made it around the world twice. On the second worldwide voyage, Captain Robert Gray decided to explore the river in the American Northwest and named it after his ship.

9. **What Davy Crockett episode was responsible for the Keel Boat attraction at Disneyland?** C. *Davy Crockett's Keelboat Race.* This episode was later spun off along with *Davy Crockett and the River Pirates* as a separate movie for theatrical release, despite the fact that Davy Crockett had died in the Alamo at the conclusion of the original, wildly popular series. The keel boat props from the movie appeared at Disneyland, giving Guests a chance to ride on actual movie props for a time, before they succumbed to age and deterioration. They were, after all, only intended for use on the TV show, not at a theme park. New keel boats debuted in 1956, and were free to roam the Rivers of America. Their design, however, made them top-heavy. After disappearing in the summer of 1994, they reappeared at the end of March, 1996. After an unfortunate capsizing in May of 1997, the Mike Fink Keel Boats were taken off the river, this time for good (they were later slated for auction on eBay.com, but did not sell and were returned to the river as background props).

10. **Which was not one of the four sections of Nature's Wonderland?** D. Cactus Alley. The others — Bear Country, Beaver Valley, the Living Desert, and Rainbow Caverns — were all different areas that the Mine Train passed through. The three outdoor sections were inspired by True-Life Adventure films of the same names, and the indoor section, Rainbow Caverns, was a holdover from the Rainbow Caverns Mine Train.

11. **Where was the Frito Kid located?** A. Casa de Fritos. This restaurant would later become Casa Mexicana. From 1955-1956, however, Casa de Fritos was located next to Aunt Jemima's

Pancake House, in the space most recently occupied by the now-defunct Wheelhouse. The Frito Kid dispensed, via a coin-operated machine, the new and popular Fritos, which were advertised as "fried tortilla" corn chips — hence the name. The Frito Kid resembled the famous "Big Boy" restaurant statues in size, shape, posture, and facial appearance, but he was able to talk via a speaker.

12. **Which is not one of the names of the landings on Tom Sawyer Island?** B. Becky's Landing. Tom's Landing, Huck's Landing, and Settler's Landing were all actual locations on the island. Tom's Landing is the only one in use by Guests today, though at one time it was possible to get to the island from two different locations on the mainland. Not all points along the river or island were themed to Mark Twain, however. Several took their names from their positions or people close to Walt. A riverboat trip would mean passing by Point Gazebo, Fowler's Harbor, Beacon Light, Point Deane, Walt's Peninsula, North Point, and Sharon Inlet.

Section Two - Medium

13. **What national park served as the inspiration for Big Thunder Mountain Railroad's towering buttes?** B. Bryce Canyon. Originally, lead designer Tony Baxter had considered the imposing cliffs of Monument Valley for a project called "Thunder Mesa" under development for Walt Disney World Resort. The attraction would house a ride called the Western River Expedition, similar to Pirates of the Caribbean (which Walt Disney World Resort did not yet have), but featuring cowboys and Indians. As it turns out, the side-project Tony was working on (Big Thunder) came to be chosen over Western River Expedition. He found the scenery too uniform and straight, however, so he turned to the towers of Bryce Canyon for inspiration, and Big Thunder Mountain Railroad was born.

The Western River Expedition idea was even older than Walt Disney World Resort, however, as it was one of the marquee attractions, together with a Haunted Mansion and a Lewis and Clark expedition, for a proposed St. Louis Disney theme park that fell through when Walt let it be known that alcohol could not be served in the park. St. Louis is home to Anheuser-Busch, and "Walt Disney's Riverfront (or alternately 'Riverboat') Square" would never be built. Florida then won out as the preferred location for the "next Disneyland."

14. **What was the original name of the canoes attraction?** F. Indian War Canoes. The name was later changed to Davy Crockett Explorer Canoes in keeping with political correctness. When the canoes debuted on July 4, 1956, they had real Indians to assist with the paddling. There had actually been motors on the first canoes, but they were heavy, and when they broke, paddling became twice as difficult. Those first wooden canoes, constructed in Maine, had been covered in canvas to give the appearance of birch, the preferred material used by Native Americans. The materials used continued to be upgraded: the second generation was wood covered with fiberglass, the third was pure fiberglass (with the paint already a part of the material), and the fourth generation was made from Kevlar.

15. **Where was Mineral Hall located?** F. Next to Casa de Fritos. This restaurant would later become Casa Mexicana and then Rancho del Zocalo. Mineral Hall, a free exhibit, showcased rocks which looked normal under daylight or normal lighting but which glowed brightly under ultraviolet or "black" lights.

16. **At one time Pepsi-Cola sponsored a restaurant in Disneyland. What location did they sponsor?** A. The Golden Horseshoe. While Coca-Cola is the official provider of soft drinks in Disneyland today, at the beginning both were available; the licensing agreements were not so strict as to shut out the competition. In fact, The Space Place Restaurant in Tomorrowland at one point served both Coca-Cola and Pepsi-Cola.

17. **During the run of the "Festival of Fools," what name did the Big Thunder Barbecue take on?** D. Festival of Foods. The name was a clever play on "Festival of Fools." The menu did not change, however, and the restaurant continued to offer barbecue amid the cluster of covered wagons.

18. **What was the name of the peak along the Rivers of America?** B. Cascade Peak. (It was sometimes referred to as Twin Sister Falls in the spiels of nearby attractions, but the official name was Cascade Peak.) The multiple waterfalls here were part of the Mine Train Through Nature's Wonderland, and in fact the original track remains there. However, in 1999 the peak was removed. It was replaced with a less kinetic grassy knoll that quickly grew lush vegetation; the original peak had fallen prey to aging, wood rot, and upkeep costs.

19. **What was the former name of the River Belle Terrace?** E. Aunt Jemima's Pancake House. It served as the original "New Orleans"-type area of Frontierland, long before New Orleans Square itself was even conceived — look up in front of the building and you can see the original 1955 facades on the upper parts reflecting the New Orleans style. An Aunt Jemima character would greet Guests outside and sign souvenir menus.

20. **What is the name of the path behind Big Thunder Mountain Railroad toward Fantasyland?** D. Big Thunder Trail. This connector between two lands opened in 1979 along with Big Thunder Mountain. The path prevented the bottleneck that had existed in this corner of Fantasyland, though it has always been one of the least populated areas of Disneyland.

21. **How many attractions in Frontierland were part of Opening Day and continue operating today?** A. One. Only the Mark Twain Riverboat was present on Opening Day. Several attractions were there on Opening Day but have since been removed: the Golden Horseshoe Revue (replaced by the Golden Horseshoe Jamboree), the Mule Pack, and the Stage Coach (both

replaced by similar attractions which were in turn themselves replaced by Big Thunder Mountain Railroad).

Section Three - Difficult

22. <u>Why is Big Thunder Mountain so named?</u> The name refers to an old Indian legend about the mountain, which would defend itself from any defacement by exacting revenge upon the interlopers. Trivia fans will remember "The Ballad of Thunder Mountain" — used in advertising the new attraction and slated for release as an LP (but never released, except on the personalized-CD "Disneyland Forever" format) — which also told the story of the mountain and its Indian history.

23. <u>What is the name of the project originally slated to connect Frontierland with Fantasyland and also mesh with the theming of Big Thunder Mountain Railroad?</u> Discovery Bay. Developed in the mid-1970s by renowned Imagineer Tony Baxter, Discovery Bay was to have been located north of Big Thunder Mountain, where instead Big Thunder Ranch moved in. The idea was to create a Gold-Rush era seaside boomtown much like San Francisco, and even offer a Chinatown area as well as a nice place to dock the Sailing Ship Columbia. Restaurants and shops would have been found at "Crossroads," the entrance to Discovery Bay, located right along the Big Thunder Trail. Though the expansion was never built, some ideas and designs from it live on: the airship design at Disneyland Paris Park's Discoveryland (note the similar name?) comes directly from the Disneyland plans. Disney's California Adventure Park borrows Discovery Bay design elements for its San Francisco and Pacific Wharf regions.

24. <u>Who christened the Mark Twain Riverboat?</u> Irene Dunne (1898-1990), noted Hollywood actress of the 1930s and 40s, did

the honors of breaking the champagne bottle on the boat during the Opening Ceremony.

25. <u>What two rides predated Big Thunder Mountain Railroad on this same plot of land?</u> In the most general sense, the answer would be the Rainbow Caverns Mine Train and the Mine Train Through Nature's Wonderland, which also used the Rainbow Caverns as its finale. However, before Big Thunder Mountain, much of this area was crisscrossed by other paths: the Stagecoach, the Conestoga Wagons, and the Pack Mules all wound their way through this stretch of property.

26. <u>Who was Mickey Moo?</u> A milk cow (she is named Mickey, but she is female) with the famous Mickey shape on her side. Austin and Linda Moore, the Maine farmers who owned her, one day discovered the mark and contacted Disneyland, who was happy to give Mickey Moo a home in Big Thunder Ranch, making her public debut on September 9, 1988 — about the same time that "State Fair" began its second year run as a Parkwide promotion. On June 7, 1990, Mickey Moo gave birth to Baby Moo, weighing 80 pounds at birth.

27. <u>Where is the Big Thunder Mountain Railroad computer room?</u> Directly behind the dinosaur skeleton. If you look closely while in line, you can see a general box-shape to the area from which the dinosaur bones jut out.

28. <u>The real stables at Disneyland are located behind the former home of Big Thunder Ranch. What is the name of this facility?</u> The Circle D Corral. This name conjures up images of Disney of course — a circle inscribing a D — but it is also a description of the brand Disneyland formerly used on its animals. These stables were started by Owen Pope, who managed the animals in the Park's earliest years. In fact, Pope's house at Circle D is the last remaining structure on the property which predates Disney's arrival. Nor is this the first time Pope was moved to the site for raising horses; when Walt was considering building his amusement park on sixteen acres of land adjacent to the Disney

Studio, he had Owen Pope move in to the property early to begin raising horses.

29. <u>Where was the hull of the Mark Twain Riverboat built?</u> Todd Shipyards in San Pedro. Both the hull of the Mark Twain Riverboat and that of the Sailing Ship Columbia were constructed at Todd Shipyards. The superstructure of the Mark Twain was built at the Disney Studios, and the two were assembled together in Fowler's Harbor during construction. Now called Todd Pacific Shipyards, the company continues as a going concern, but operates out of its Seattle location and no longer has facilities in San Pedro.

30. <u>Who provided the narration for the Mine Train Through Nature's Wonderland attraction?</u> Dallas McKennon. For Disney, McKennon also lent his voice for the safety warning on the Mine Train's replacement, Big Thunder Mountain Railroad. McKennon's voice has been used in many animated features and shorts, including the claymation show "Gumby."

31. <u>What 8 flags fly over the Riverboat Dock?</u> The flags flown over the dock are from various periods of America's history. The first is Old Glory (24 stars and 13 stripes) — first hoisted above a ship in 1831; the Star Spangled Banner (15 stars and 15 stripes) — the flag that inspired the national anthem of the same name; the Betsy Ross Flag (13 stars and 13 stripes) — the first official American flag; the Grand Union Flag — first raised by George Washington in 1776; the Pine Tree Flag — the first flag carried by the American Navy; the Continental Flag — carried by the American troops at Bunker Hill; the King's Colors Flag — the flag flown while the colonies were being founded; and the John Cabot Flag — the first flag flown on the American mainland.

32. <u>What is the target year for Frontierland's theme?</u> 1860. Walt once fumed that a car belonging to a lazy photographer was visible from the Mark Twain Riverboat, and it was destroying the integrity of the theming set in 1860. Originally, the Frontierland era extended from approximately 1790 to 1876,

and was represented in different parts of the land, like the Stockade entrance area representing the Revolutionary period and the Mexican area depicting the Southwest of around the 1850s.

33. <u>**What are the names of the Big Thunder Mountain Railroad trains?**</u> U.R. Courageous, I.M. Brave, I.M. Bold, U.R. Fearless, I.B. Hearty, and U.R. Daring — all wordplays that inform the sharp-eyed visitor that this ride will not be gentle! The safety spiel created for the ride drove the point home: "Howdy folks! Please keep your hands, arms and legs inside the train and remain seated at all times. Now then, hang on to them hats an' glasses, 'cause this here's the wildest ride in the wilderness!"

Adventureland

Adventureland Questions

Section One - Easy

1. What is the newest attraction in Adventureland?
    - a. Indiana Jones Adventure
    - b. Tarzan's Treehouse
    - c. Aladdin's Oasis
    - d. Enchanted Tiki Room

2. What is the waterfall in the Jungle Cruise called?
    - a. Schweitzer Falls
    - b. Twin Sister Falls
    - c. Jungle Falls
    - d. Adventureland Falls

3. What song serves as exit music to the Enchanted Tiki Room show?
    - a. "Baroque Hoedown"
    - b. "Pele's Revenge"
    - c. "Hawaiian War Chant"
    - d. "Heigh-Ho"

4. Who is <u>not</u> one of the four stars of the Enchanted Tiki Room?
   a. Jose
   b. Fritz
   c. Michael
   d. David

5. What is Trader Sam's Daily Special?
   a. Two heads for one of yours
   b. Two heads for one of his
   c. Three heads for one of yours
   d. Three of your heads for his

6. What are the first words spoken in the Enchanted Tiki Room?
   a. "Buenos dias, señor"
   b. "Buenos dias, señorita"
   c. "Buenos dias, mis amigos"
   d. "Buenos dias, monsieur"

7. Who is the "father of all gods and goddesses?"
   a. Rongo
   b. Pele
   c. Tangaroa-Ru
   d. Tangaroa

8. What restaurant preceded Aladdin's Oasis?
   a. Tiki Terrace
   b. Tahitian Terrace
   c. Hawaiian Terrace
   d. Adventureland Terrace

9. What room was not a part of the Swiss Family Treehouse?
   a. Kitchen
   b. Kids' Bedroom
   c. Library
   d. Greenhouse

10. Adventureland was conceived as a showcase for which type of film made by the Disney Studios in the 1950s?
    a. Studio Package genre films
    b. Laugh-O-grams
    c. True-Life Adventures
    d. Silly Symphonies

11. What walk-up restaurant did the Bengal Barbecue replace?
    a. Sunkist, I Presume
    b. Swift, I Presume
    c. Starkist, I Presume
    d. Sunrise, I Presume

12. What is the name of the evil god in the Indiana Jones Adventure?
    a. Ra
    b. Cthulu
    c. Kaa
    d. Mara

13. What is the main booby trap in the queue area for the Indiana Jones Adventure?
     a. Falling boulders
     b. Tumbling crates
     c. Falling ceiling of spikes
     d. Tumbling bricks

14. What is written in strange font above the side-by-side drinking fountains in the Indy queue?
     a. "Choose wisely"
     b. "Mara's fountain"
     c. "Drink, thirsty travelers"
     d. "Do not touch"

15. What recent Disney film is honored at the base of Tarzan's Treehouse?
     a. *The Lion King*
     b. *Beauty and the Beast*
     c. *The Little Mermaid*
     d. *Aladdin*

Section Two - Medium

16. When it was first constructed, the artificial tree on the Tahitian Terrace stage was too short. How did they solve the problem?
     a. Re-shape the viewing area

b. Buy lowered tables and chairs
c. Add concrete to the top of the tree
d. Add concrete to the middle of the tree
e. Start over with a new tree
f. Raise the entire stage

17. How did the Tiki Room generate business in the early days?
   a. Jungle Cruise closed early
   b. Discount pricing
   c. Barker bird outside entrance
   d. Belly dancers
   e. Plaza Pavilion Cast Members wore Tiki Room costumes
   f. Volume on queue area speakers turned up

18. Which scene was added to the Jungle Cruise in 1962?
   a. Elephant Bathing Pool
   b. Water Buffalo
   c. Trader Sam
   d. Village of Natives
   e. Hippo Pool
   f. Schweitzer Falls

19. Where could one find a reference to the ship "Titus" in Adventureland?
   a. Indiana Jones Adventure
   b. Swiss Family Treehouse

c. River Belle Terrace

d. Aladdin's Oasis

e. Enchanted Tiki Room

f. Tropical Imports

20. In what Southern California city were the
Jungle Cruise boats assembled?

    a. Costa Mesa

    b. Newport Beach

    c. Long Beach

    d. Irvine

    e. Anaheim

    f. Los Angeles

21. What song was removed from
Disneyland's Enchanted Tiki Room in
1996?

    a. "Hawaiian War Chant"

    b. "Heigh-Ho"

    c. "Hawaiian Luau"

    d. "The Tiki, Tiki, Tiki Room"

    e. "Offenbach's Barcarolle"

    f. "Let's All Sing (Like the Birdies
Sing)"

22. How many theoretical ride variations are
there in the Indiana Jones Adventure?

    a. 1

    b. 3

    c. 15

    d. 999

e. 15,000

f. 160,000

Section Three - Difficult

23. Why was a British flag added to the Jungle Cruise in 1994?

24. Who is "Bones"?

25. What was the original concept for an Indiana Jones ride in Adventureland?

26. Which presidential press secretary used to work on the Jungle Cruise?

27. Where did the "Little Man of Disneyland" live?

28. What Enchanted Tiki Room bird did Golden Horseshoe Revue star Wally Boag voice?

29. What company was going to sponsor the Enchanted Tiki Room when it was supposed to be a restaurant?

Adventureland
Answers

Section One - Easy

1. <u>What is the newest attraction in Adventureland?</u> B. Tarzan's Treehouse. This walkthrough, which replaced the aging Swiss Family Treehouse, opened in 1999. Only four years earlier its next-door neighbor, the Indiana Jones Adventure, was "excavated."

2. <u>What is the waterfall in the Jungle Cruise called?</u> A. Schweitzer Falls. Walt hated this structure because it required so much expensive cement while the Park was being built, and he was running out of money. The standard joke is that it is named after that famous African explorer, "Dr. Albert Falls."

3. <u>What song serves as exit music to the Enchanted Tiki Room show?</u> D. "Heigh-Ho." However, the lyrics are altered: "Heigh-ho, heigh-ho, it's out the door you go!" It is preceded by the "Hawaiian War Chant [with Angry Tiki Gods]," a song that, like most tunes in the Tiki Room, existed long before Disneyland. That is followed by a quick reprise of the Tiki Room original music, written by the Sherman Brothers, and then the version of "Heigh-Ho" serves as exit music. The War Chant marks the debut of the wooden tiki drummers along the ceiling and the creepy tiki masks along the walls, but eventually all the birds and plants join in

until the entire room's Audio-Animatronics are singing along.

4. <u>Who is not one of the four stars of the Enchanted Tiki Room?</u> D. David. The four macaw stars, originally known as "MacAudios" in the attraction's training manual, are: Fritz, the German; Pierre, the Frenchman; Jose, the Spaniard; and Michael, the Irishman. Of the rest of the birds, only the female cockatoos have names: Colette, Suzette, Mimi, Gigi, Fifi, and Josephine.

5. <u>What is Trader Sam's Daily Special?</u> A. He will sell you "two of his heads for one of yours." Trader Sam first made his appearance along the jungle river in 1957, and his section of the jungle is meant to represent the Amazon.

6. <u>What are the first words spoken in the Enchanted Tiki Room?</u> B. "Buenos días, señorita." The host or hostess taps Jose to wake him up, and Jose says, after a yawn, "Buenos días, señorita." Clever male hosts sometimes cue the taped speech by cautioning Jose not to call him "señorita" this time, but of course he always does.

7. <u>Who is the "father of all gods and goddesses?"</u> D. Tangaroa. This "father," from whose limbs "new life shall fall," is the large (artificial) tree near the Enchanted Tiki Room entrance and the last of the gods/goddesses to speak in the Tiki Room pre-show before Guests are allowed in the theater. Tangaroa is the Polynesian god of the ocean, and as such is often associated with fertility. Other Gods include Maui, who "roped the playful sun and gave his people time"; Koro, the "Midnight Dancer"; Tangaroa-Ru, "Goddess of the East Wind"; Hina Kuluna, "Goddess of the Rain"; Pele, "Goddess of Fire and Volcano"; Ngendei, "The Earth Balancer"; and Rongo, "God of Agriculture."

8. **What restaurant preceded Aladdin's Oasis?** B. Tahitian Terrace. This dinner theater included a free show set in the South Seas with each meal, featuring Polynesian-style entertainment. While the Tahitian Terrace was popular with Guests, its dinner-show format and table service made it less profitable than other locations, and the success of the movie *Aladdin* seemed to offer a chance to infuse some positive change into the stale Adventureland in 1993. At first, Aladdin's Oasis attempted a similar style service with a stage show, but its attendance and sales began slipping, and the show was abandoned for a pure table-service restaurant. The new establishment featured, amusingly, servers with "exaggerated personalities": one might play forgetful, another might act like he is hard of hearing, and so on. Alas, this too failed to excite the Guests, and the location fell into disuse before being revived as a storytelling location.

9. **What room was not at the Swiss Family Treehouse?** D. Greenhouse. The Kitchen, the Library, the Recreation Room (with pipe organ), the Parents' room, and the Crow's nest (bedroom of the Robinson kids), were all represented. The continuously playing music, the "Swisskapolka," was scored for the film by Buddy Baker and could be heard throughout the attraction and, on a quiet night, all through the rest of the Park.

10. **Adventureland was conceived as a showcase for which type of film made by the Disney Studios in the 1950s?** C. True-Life Adventures. This new style of documentary helped save the studio from insolvency directly following the war (and won Walt eight Academy Awards). These films went to exotic locales in the world and observed, though some would say interacted with, the animals there. Originally, Walt had wanted live animals in the Jungle Cruise, but he was quickly advised that live animals would be both

dangerous and apt to be asleep during Park hours. The only live animals in the Jungle Cruise would be alligators in the queue, borrowed from a Buena Park facility, but these too were given up quickly because they would get sick on popcorn or escape into the waters of the Jungle Cruise, where handlers would have to track them down and capture them.

11. **What walk-up restaurant did the Bengal Barbecue replace?** A. Sunkist, I Presume. This location was a lessee/participant, run by Sunkist rather than by Disneyland. From 1958 until 1989, Sunkist also operated the Sunkist Citrus House on Main Street, in the current home of the Gibson Girl Ice Cream Parlor. When their lease expired in 1990, both locations closed; the Adventureland location was replaced by the Bengal Barbecue and the Blue Ribbon Bakery replaced the Main Street locale before moving next door in 1997.

12. **What's the name of the evil god in the Indiana Jones Adventure?** D. Mara. Legend tells us that we cannot look into the eyes of Mara or we will befall his curse, which of course is death. Naturally, we are given no choice in the matter, as we are steered directly at a statue of the god, and we cannot help but look.

13. **What is the main booby trap in the queue area for the Indiana Jones Adventure?** C. Falling ceiling of spikes. The most obvious booby trap is the bamboo pole which triggers a falling ceiling, complete with spikes in the descending ceiling and floor. When the ride was new, this effect was louder and more startling, and the ceiling dropped rather violently toward the Guests. However, it was perhaps too realistic for some Guests, so it was toned down. The bamboo pole is frequently mistreated by some more zealous Guests who do not understand that the effect needs time to reset itself, so it is sometimes not functional. The rope near a well is

interactive, too; if you tug it, the archeologists below will speak one of several set phrases. The diamond shaped floor tiles just after the spike room do not trigger another booby trap, though such a trap is hinted at, with the ceiling blocks wedged into place with mere wood slivers. The line moves very quickly, and most Guests do not have a chance to enjoy the subtlety that is already present.

14. **What is written in strange font above the side-by-side drinking fountains in the Indy queue?** A. "Choose wisely." The reference is both to the third Indiana Jones movie and to the tagline for the original sponsor AT&T. The phone company's use of the phrase is obvious — choose them over competitors — but it's the movie's use of the phrase which renders its appearance here funny. In *Indiana Jones and the Last Crusade*, anyone who stumbles upon the keeper of the Holy Grail sees a dizzying array of cups and chalices to choose from. He who chooses correctly gets eternal life, but an incorrect choice results in death. You can only choose once, and you must drink from the cup you choose. The implication is that one of these fountains at the Indy ride will dispense the water of Life (though of course the other isn't poisonous; that wouldn't be very hospitable to kill the Guests!) The full text at the drinking fountain reads: "Only one spring will restore youth and vigor. Choose wisely." This type of font, by the way, is called alternately Mara font, Maraglyphics, or Marascript.

15. **What recent Disney film is honored at the base of Tarzan's Treehouse?** B. *Beauty and the Beast.* At the base of the tree is a table with a large, rounded teapot and a little cup, both with the distinctive colored trim that the characters Mrs. Potts and Chip had from the film. In case there was any doubt, the little teacup even has a chip in its rim.

Section Two - Medium

16. <u>When it was first constructed, the artificial tree on the Tahitian Terrace stage was too short. How did they solve the problem?</u> D. Add concrete to the middle of the tree. At Walt's suggestion, they simply cut through the tree in the middle and added concrete to make it taller. Bill Martin, then art director at Disneyland, saw to it that the trunk was then raised four feet. The problem arose because the trunk was built on location, while the limbs were built in the Staff Shop backstage. When they attached the limbs, they quickly noticed that they hung too low and obstructed the performers and stage lighting. The tree was finally removed in 2005.

17. <u>How did the Tiki Room generate business in the early days?</u> C. Barker bird outside entrance. An additional copy of the macaw Jose was created to serve as a "barker bird" outside the Enchanted Tiki Room, to let Guests know what to expect inside (this was necessary since Audio-Animatronics were simply unheard-of in those days, and the Tiki Room was the first such attraction). He had to be removed, however, because flabbergasted Guests would stop below the bird and clog up the Adventureland bridge, too entertained at the free show (this was in the days of coupons for rides) to move on. This bird was found in storage 17 years later, cleaned, and put back into the show as a "side macaw" in the 1980s.

18. <u>Which scene was added to the Jungle Cruise in 1962?</u> A. Elephant Bathing Pool. A new loading structure was also created, and there was new landscaping for the

African Veldt area as well. Adventureland received a major makeover in 1962 to prepare for the opening of both the Swiss Family Treehouse and the Enchanted Tiki Room. (It was a slight embarrassment to Disneyland that the Tiki Room wasn't ready on time, and instead opened a year later.) The original two story loading structure (basically one story with a lookout post on top) received a single story replacement, which was in turn replaced in 1994 in another Adventureland refurbishment, in preparation for the opening of the Indiana Jones Adventure. While Imagineering's efforts in the years before 1964 were devoted to the New York World's Fair, the African Veldt and Elephant Bathing Pool areas were landscaped ahead of time in preparation for the arrival of the figures (which were installed in 1964).

19. **Where could one find a reference to the ship "Titus" in Adventureland?** Swiss Family Treehouse. This was the name of the ship upon which the family had been traveling when they were shipwrecked. Interestingly, at one time the sign telling of the family's troubles listed the ship name as that of the "Recovery." Apparently, the Robinsons couldn't remember which ship they had sailed on!

20. **In what Southern California city were the Jungle Cruise boats assembled?** B. Costa Mesa. The original Jungle Cruise boats were designed by Harper Goff and ran on natural gas. The boats are stored overnight in a slip canal between the Jungle Cruise and the backside of Main Street; you can see the area leading off to the canal right next to Aladdin's Oasis.

21. **What song was removed from Disneyland's Enchanted Tiki Room in 1996?** A. "Offenbach's Barcarolle." This song, taken from the "Tales of Hoffmann," originally followed the introductory chorus of the "The Tiki, Tiki,

Tiki Room" and preceded the magical fountain and female cockatoos. It was removed to shorten, and thus tighten, the show in an effort to stop walkouts by Guests. The revised show indeed zips right along and no longer suffers from the walkouts it once did.

22. **How many theoretical ride variations are there in the Indiana Jones Adventure?** F. 160,000. The easy answer is three, if you were thinking of the different doorways at the beginning, which lead to Eternal Youth, Earthly Riches, or Future Knowledge. However, the correct answer is closer to 160,000. Each transport is equipped with an onboard computer, which randomly recombines several ride elements into different orders and locations. For example, on most rides your transport will breakdown at some point, but it might happen in the bug room, on the bridge, the rat room, or in the dark room before the darts. The Indy Audio-Animatronics figure will also vary what he says to you, the snake lunges at different areas of the car, the stone god will shoot fireballs at different areas and times, and so on. The result is a slightly different ride each time you visit the attraction, guaranteeing its freshness.

Section Three - Difficult

23. **Why was a British flag added to the Jungle Cruise in 1994?** According to a new theme installed in 1994, the Jungle Trading Company, which offers us the "jungle cruise" we embark upon, has its Home Office at 70 Thames Road, in London. So the entire operation is a British one, and our trek through the jungle is meant to convey the sense of British colonialism.

24. **Who is "Bones"?** As another inside joke by Imagineers, one of the skeletons in the first Skeleton Room of the Indiana Jones Adventure was decorated with Mickey Ears such as can be bought throughout the Park. This skeleton is hard to find, however; he is in the alcove to your left as you first skid into the skeleton area and you will have to twist around almost backward to find him. He is next to the wall painting of another odd character in the ride, the Skeleton King, who is crowned and seated on a throne.

25. **What was the original concept for an Indiana Jones ride in Adventureland?** The initial concept called for not one ride, but two: a jeep transport ride such as we have now (if a bit tamer), and a mine-car chase that would resemble a roller coaster, as inspired by the sequence in *Indiana Jones and the Temple of Doom*. (A mine-car roller coaster similar to that envisioned for Disneyland in California was built for Disneyland Paris Park.) In fact, the same sort of overlapping view we enjoy of Splash Mountain from the Disneyland Railroad was also proposed for Indy, with both the Jungle Cruise and the Disneyland Railroad skirting by a grand central chamber in which the two new kinetic rides would be visible. When the project was scaled back to one ride, the transports benefited by becoming "simulator-enhanced" to turbo-charge the experience. The attraction was spearheaded by Imagineers Skip Lange and Susan Bonds, based on renderings and ideas by Herb Ryman and Tony Baxter. Dave Durham programmed the transports used in the attractions, as well as the ones in Dinosaur (a similar attraction at Walt Disney World Resort, then named Countdown to Extinction) and Cosmic Waves, the interactive fountain in Tomorrowland.

26. **Which presidential press secretary used to work on the Jungle Cruise?** Richard Nixon's press secretary Ron

Ziegler. On one visit to Disneyland by then-president Nixon and his entourage, Ziegler was given permission to take out one of the boats and try to give the spiel himself many years later.

27. **Where did the "Little Man of Disneyland" live?** In a tree near the Jungle Cruise. The Little Man of Disneyland, a leprechaun named Patrick Begorra, was an invention in 1955 by The Walt Disney Company to advertise the new Park via the popular book series Little Golden Books, which continue to delight children today. Supposedly this leprechaun lived on the land before Disneyland was even built. A tree trunk in Adventureland was partly hollowed out, and Guests could peer into it to see his home, complete with miniaturized furnishings. Because the public's memory is short, the hollowed trunk soon lost its meaning and the hole was filled up — but the tree stayed in Disneyland until September 2001! If you looked closely at the tree nearest the Jungle Cruise entrance, you found the cement-filled knot — maybe six inches across — that was once the home of the Little Man of Disneyland.

28. **What Enchanted Tiki Room bird did Golden Horseshoe Revue star Wally Boag voice?** Jose. Fellow Golden Horseshoe star Fulton Burley voiced Michael; Thurl Ravenscroft, a prolific Disneyland voice actor, voiced Fritz; and then-famous voice actor Dr. Horatio Q. Birdbath (his legal name!), lent his voice as that of Pierre. Birdbath also did all the bird tweets and whistles for the show.

29. **What company was going to sponsor the Enchanted Tiki Room when it was supposed to be a restaurant?** Stouffer's. Walt's original idea was to offer a kind of dinner-theater, where the performance would be 100% composed of Audio-Animatronics birds. The idea

proved cost-inefficient, and the restaurant idea was scrapped in favor of a show, which could move people through more quickly (and thus make more money in the days of attractions tickets). One facility remains from the original restaurant concept, however — the little known bathrooms in the Tiki Room waiting area were installed for the proposed dining establishment.

New Orleans Square

New Orleans Square Questions

Section One - Easy

1. Finish this phrase in the Haunted Mansion: "Hurry Back! Hurry Back! Be sure to bring your _____."
   a. Final arrangements
   b. Birth certificate
   c. Death certificate
   d. Driver's License

2. What is the name of the restaurant that boats travel past in the Pirates of the Caribbean?
   a. Blue Lagoon
   b. Blue Moon
   c. Blue Bayou
   d. Blue Swamp

3. What is the name of the pirate-themed shop at the exit to the Pirates of the Caribbean?
   a. Swashbucklers
   b. Doubloons!
   c. The Treasure Chest
   d. Pieces of Eight

4. What is the five-word motto of the Pirates of the Caribbean?
    a. Pirates rule the world forever
    b. A pirate's life for me
    c. We plunder and we loot
    d. Dead folks keep our secret

5. How many ghosts inhabit the Haunted Mansion?
    a. 47
    b. 52
    c. 68
    d. 999

6. What song is the old man at the shack in the bayou playing on his banjo, as you pass by on the Pirates attraction?
    a. "Star-Spangled Banner"
    b. "Yo Ho (A Pirate's Life for Me)"
    c. "Oh, Susanna"
    d. "Whistling Dixie"

7. At which restaurant does the jazz ensemble play at an outdoor stage?
    a. Royal Street Veranda
    b. Blue Bayou
    c. Café Orleans
    d. French Market

8. What immediately follows this quote at the start of the Haunted Mansion: "When hinges creak in doorless chambers…"?
    a. "And strange and frightening sounds echo through the halls"
    b. "That is the time when ghosts are present"
    c. "Whenever candlelights flicker"
    d. "Hurry back"

9. What have we seen that makes the disembodied voice in Pirates of the Caribbean think we know too much?
    a. The pirates' treasure
    b. The pirate ship attacking the fort
    c. The auction of women
    d. The burning city

10. What do the drunken Pirates at the auction want?
    a. Gold
    b. Rum
    c. The Redhead
    d. Chickens

11. In the Haunted Mansion, where was the Hatbox Ghost?
    a. Graveyard
    b. Attic
    c. Ballroom
    d. Hitchhiking

12. What is the name of the members-only club in New Orleans Square?
    a. Westside Diner
    b. Inn Between
    c. Company D
    d. Club 33

13. What was the Disney Gallery designed to be?
    a. Walt's new apartment in the Park
    b. A second Disneyana shop
    c. An art gallery
    d. A preview center for Disneyland expansions

14. What is the Haunted Mansion ride system called?
    a. Gravity boat ride
    b. PeopleMover
    c. Omnimover
    d. Ghostmover

15. How can the Haunted Mansion and Pirates of the Caribbean fit into such small spaces inside Disneyland?
    a. They go very deep underground
    b. They take us outside the normal boundaries of the Park

c. Guests are shrunk
d. They overlap each other on
    three stories

Section Two - Medium

16. What were the first two exhibitions to
    show in the Disney Gallery?
    a. "The Art of Disneyland 1953-
        1986" and "Looking at the
        Future — Tomorrowland: 1955-
        1998"
    b. "The Art of Disneyland 1953-
        1986" and "35 Years of Disney
        Dreams"
    c. "The Art of the Indiana Jones
        Adventure" and "Looking at the
        Future — Tomorrowland: 1955-
        1998"
    d. "The Art of the Indiana Jones
        Adventure" and "The Art of
        Disneyland 1953-1986"
    e. "Looking at the Future —
        Tomorrowland: 1955-1998" and
        "35 Years of Disney Dreams"
    f. "Looking at the Future —
        Tomorrowland: 1955-1998" and
        "The Art of Disneyland Paris"

17. The success of what Disney film allowed
    Walt the resources to get Pirates of the
    Caribbean built?
        a. *Peter Pan*
        b. *Bambi*
        c. *Sleeping Beauty*
        d. *Cinderella*
        e. *Mary Poppins*
        f. *The Love Bug*

18. What Walt Disney Imagineer came up
    with most of the visual effects in the
    Haunted Mansion?
        a. Claude Coats
        b. Marc Davis
        c. Blaine Gibson
        d. Thurl Ravenscroft
        e. Chris Mueller
        f. Yale Gracey

19. The exclusive restaurant in New Orleans
    Square contains a phone booth from what
    Disney movie?
        a. *Mary Poppins*
        b. *That Darn Cat!*
        c. *The Happiest Millionaire*
        d. *Son of Flubber*
        e. *Blackbeard's Ghost*
        f. *The Love Bug*

20. Why was a spider design added to one glass pane at the ballroom scene of the Haunted Mansion?

    a. To cover up a bullet hole in the glass

    b. Then-chairman of Disney, Card Walker, had spiders as pets

    c. Spiders continually infest the ballroom

    d. To promote the Disney movie *Arachnophobia*

    e. To add realism to the scene

    f. Surveys showed children wanted the attraction to be scarier

21. What was the sentimental reason behind installing an antiques store (The One-of-a-Kind Shop) in New Orleans Square?

    a. Walt bought every antique he could find

    b. Walt's daughters wanted to manage the store

    c. Walt's wife Lillian collected antiques

    d. Walt's mother insisted upon it

    e. Roy and his wife demanded an antiques store

    f. There was no sentimental reason

22. What part of New Orleans Square was conceived of, and partly built, long before it was finished and opened?
    a. Haunted Mansion
    b. One-of-a-Kind Shop
    c. Blue Bayou
    d. Club 33
    e. French Market
    f. Café Orleans

23. Whose face is on the broken statue in the graveyard scene of the Haunted Mansion?
    a. Walt Disney
    b. Roy O. Disney
    c. Thurl Ravenscroft
    d. Jack Wagner
    e. Mike Wagner
    f. Yale Gracey

24. Who wrote the lyrics for "Yo Ho (A Pirate's Life for Me)" for Pirates of the Caribbean?
    a. George Bruns
    b. X. Atencio
    c. The Sherman Brothers
    d. Buddy Baker
    e. Fess Parker
    f. Walt Disney

25. Who wrote the music for "Yo Ho (A Pirate's Life for Me)"?
   a. George Bruns
   b. X. Atencio
   c. The Sherman Brothers
   d. Buddy Baker
   e. Fess Parker
   f. Walt Disney

26. Who penned the lyrics to "Grim Grinning Ghosts"?
   a. George Bruns
   b. X. Atencio
   c. The Sherman Brothers
   d. Buddy Baker
   e. Fess Parker
   f. Walt Disney

Section Three - Difficult

27. What are the various ways Haunted Mansion ghosts are generated?

28. What is the history of the hearse in front of the Haunted Mansion?

29. How much did New Orleans Square cost to build?

30. Which 1985 theatrical movie had been inspired, particularly in its set design, directly from the Pirates of the Caribbean?

31. Who provided the voice for the Ghost Host?

32. How did the Trophy Room in Club 33 get its name?

33. Who designed the costumes for the pirates in the Pirates of the Caribbean?

New Orleans Square Answers

Section One - Easy

1. <u>Finish this phrase: "Hurry Back! Hurry Back! Be sure to bring your ...."</u> C. Death certificate. The full quote is: "Hurry Back! Hurry Back! Be sure to bring your death certificate, if you decide to join us. Make final arrangements now. We've been… dying to have you." This is Little Leota, heard as you ascend the final speedramp exiting the Haunted Mansion. The face and billowy dress projected on a small statuette have always been a source of fascination, utilizing the face and voice of Imagineer Leota Toombs, who is also the face of Madame Leota in the Mansion's seance scene (but not the voice; that is Eleanor Audley, the actress who played Maleficent in *Sleeping Beauty* and Lady Tremaine in *Cinderella*).

2. <u>What is the name of the restaurant that boats travel past in the Pirates of the Caribbean?</u> C. Blue Bayou. This famous restaurant has received a few Silver Palm awards for culinary excellence in its time, and its mood was set by none less than Walt Disney, who shortly before his death decreed that the lighting and other designs be changed to reflect the proper atmosphere. This was one of the last instances of Walt's famous stance for quality and showmanship over profit, as the restaurant was otherwise ready for business and could have been earning money much sooner. It would not open until the rest of the complex was ready, including Pirates of the Caribbean, just months after his death.

3. <u>What is the name of the pirate-themed shop at the exit to the Pirates of the Caribbean?</u> D. Pieces of Eight. This name refers to the silver coins common on the Spanish Main in the 18th

century. Guests can purchase a personalized "piece of eight" from a machine in the shop, or peruse the other pirate-themed merchandise.

4. <u>What is the five-word motto of the Pirates of the Caribbean?</u> B. A pirate's life for me. There are actually two answers to this question: both "A Pirate's Life for Me" and "Dead Men Tell No Tales" qualify as mottos for the attraction. The latter phrase appears in the monologue of the skull-and-crossbones before the first drop, in the eerily dark tunnel before the battle scene, and as we ascend the waterfall at the end. Naturally, you can find it on numerous T-shirts and assorted merchandise in the Pirate-themed shop, Pieces of Eight, that you encounter at the ride's exit. The other motto can be heard throughout the attraction in the theme song and can also be found on Pieces of Eight souvenirs.

5. <u>How many ghosts inhabit the Haunted Mansion?</u> D. 999. However, we are told by the welcoming plaque that "there is always room for a thousand!" implying that if we were bold — or foolish — enough, we might join the ranks of the permanent residents of the mansion. This joking threat is a consistent one in the storyline; we are told by the Ghost Host after the stretching portraits that if we "insist on lagging behind, you may not need to volunteer [to remain]" and by Little Leota that we should hurry back, as the ghosts here are "dying" to have us.

6. <u>What song is the old man at the shack in the bayou playing on his banjo, as you pass by on the Pirates attraction?</u> C. "Oh, Susanna." The tune is played much slower than is customary, in order to fully set the mood of the bayou — laid back, with time at a standstill. The unintended result is that many patrons find the music familiar but not exactly recognizable. "Camptown Races" was another song recorded for this spot, but it is no longer used.

7. <u>At which restaurant does the jazz ensemble play at an outdoor stage?</u> D. The French Market. The group which performs at the

stage most often is the Side Street Strutters, and they also play on one of the rafts as a pre-show before Fantasmic in the evenings. In the 1960s, it wasn't unusual to find the Firehouse Five Plus Two — led by Disney animator Ward Kimball — playing here.

8. <u>**What immediately follows this quote at the start of the Haunted Mansion: "When hinges creak in doorless chambers…"?**</u> A. "And strange and frightening sounds echo through the halls." This is the opening sentence of the Haunted Mansion's soundtrack, told to Guests as they assemble before entering the portrait gallery: "When hinges creak in doorless chambers, and strange and frightening sounds echo through the halls; whenever candlelights flicker, where the air is deathly still — that is the time when ghosts are present, practicing their terror with ghoulish delight."

9. <u>**What have we seen that makes the disembodied voice in Pirates of the Caribbean think we know too much?**</u> A. The pirates' treasure. We are told that "perhaps ye knows too much; ye seen the cursed treasure." This monologue and in fact the entire darkened passage with the disembodied voice is not found at the Pirates attraction in Walt Disney World Resort or in the international versions, for two reasons: first, in those incarnations we do not see the looted riches until the end of the ride (the set elements are ordered differently); and second, we do not need to travel outside the berm at those Parks, since Pirates was part of their initial overall design!

10. <u>**What do the drunken Pirates at the auction want?**</u> C. The Redhead. The auctioneer is trying to sell off a "winsome wench," but the drunken pirates ridicule her weight and instead chant "We wants the redhead!" until a disgruntled pirate fires off a warning shot for them to behave. The Auctioneer is one of the most advanced Audio-Animatronics in the Park and the first new-generation AA to debut.

11. **In the Haunted Mansion, where was the Hatbox Ghost?** B. Attic. The Hatbox Ghost was a ghost from the attic scene of the Haunted Mansion, but it was an effect that didn't work well and was removed almost immediately. He was so named because his head would disappear from atop his shoulders, only to reappear, via lighting effects, in the hatbox he carried in his hand. Descriptions of him appeared on promotional 33 1/3 records created for the attraction's opening and sold for many years thereafter.

12. **What is the name of the members-only club in New Orleans Square?** D. Club 33. The name refers just to its address on Royal Street at Disneyland (the common explanation, that there were thirty-three original lessees at the park, is incorrect). This is the one place in Disneyland which serves alcohol, but membership is very expensive and requires waiting for years on the list before it is offered. The restaurant covers much of the visible second story of the whole land of New Orleans Square (it's technically the third floor, since the apparent ground level of the land is in reality already the second story, with the attraction and backstage areas occupying the real ground floor). The entrance to Club 33 is next to the Blue Bayou, with the reception area directly above. From there, the Trophy Room dining area extends over the Bayou and beyond, with the kitchen beyond that extending virtually to the Disney Gallery. The hallway from the reception area to the other dining room crosses over Royal Street, with the main dining room situated over Café Orleans. The areas over the French Market and remaining sections of New Orleans are office and storerooms.

13. **What was the Disney Gallery designed to be?** A. Walt's new apartment. His old one atop the Firehouse on Main Street simply wasn't big enough for visitors or even his entire family. Unfortunately, he died before work was completed, and the area was used as office space and storage until it opened as the Disney Gallery in 1987.

14. <u>What is the Haunted Mansion ride system called?</u> C. Omnimovers. These vehicles are here known as Doom Buggies, or so we are told by the Ghost Host just before the loading area. This system was first used in Adventure Thru Inner Space, and proved so popular with the designers that it was used again at the Haunted Mansion. The clamshells could move large numbers of people quickly and safely, and best of all, the vehicles could be turned at the designer's will to view whatever they found important. This extended the Imagineers' ability to tell a story by focusing Guests' attention on certain elements; in a way, it fused together the linear storytelling of filmed sequences with the advantages of a three-dimensional environment, and captured the best of both worlds.

15. <u>How can the Haunted Mansion and Pirates of the Caribbean fit into such small spaces inside Disneyland?</u> B. They take us outside the normal boundaries of the park. They descend underground — actually to ground level; the rest of New Orleans Square is actually the "second floor" — and proceed under the berm which surrounds Disneyland. In the Mansion, you proceed under the berm as you walk down the hallway with the changing portraits, and in Pirates you enter the show building outside the berm as you pass through the darkened tunnel filled with warnings and enter the battle scene between the pirate ship and the fort. You also cross under the berm at Indiana Jones and Splash Mountain, by the way: at Indy it happens during the Bat Cave and Spike Room and in Splash Mountain you travel <u>over</u> the berm just after the first drop. If you watch carefully you can see that you enter a building just after that drop. Mickey's Toontown and "it's a small world" also lie outside the berm, but in more obvious ways.

Section Two - Medium

16. <u>What were the first two exhibitions to show in the Disney Gallery?</u> B. "The Art of Disneyland 1953-1986" and "35 Years of Disney Dreams." The first was "The Art of Disneyland 1953-1986," which opened with the Gallery in 1987, showcasing many of the Imagineering designs and sketches for the Park. The second, opened on November 23, 1989, was "35 Years of Disney Dreams," a re-consideration of the first theme, with emphasis on "The Disneyland That Never Was."

17. <u>The success of what Disney film allowed Walt the resources to get Pirates of the Caribbean built?</u> E. *Mary Poppins.* The 1964 film garnered several Oscars, including Best Actress, Best Score and Best Song, and provided a wealth of income for the Disney Studios right when work on New Orleans Square was commencing. While the attraction itself wasn't in jeopardy, the revenue generated by the movie allowed Walt to make it to perfection, something he always strove for. It was this perfection that kept him from seeing the finished product; he didn't want the public to see a substandard attraction and therefore delayed its opening. It was the last attraction Walt was vigorously involved in.

18. <u>What Walt Disney Imagineer came up with most of the visual effects in the Haunted Mansion?</u> F. Yale Gracey. Yale had also come up with the technology used for the burning city of the Pirates of the Caribbean, though it took Claude Coats' notice of Gracey's effect to have it installed.

19. <u>Club 33, the exclusive restaurant in New Orleans Square, contains a phone booth from what Disney movie?</u> C. *The Happiest Millionaire.* The soda fountain for many years in Café Orleans was also used in the 1967 movie, for which Walt had had high hopes. Though the movie has faded from memory, portions of its props continue to exist at these two Disneyland locations.

20. <u>Why was a spider design added to one glass pane at the ballroom scene of the Haunted Mansion?</u> A. To cover up a bullet hole in the glass. The blemish had apparently been created by a Guest with an illegal firearm, probably a BB gun. There were similar holes in the glass sets at the Adventure Thru Inner Space and the Disneyland Railroad dioramas; someone apparently went on a shooting rampage in 1978 at Disneyland! The incident occurred during a private party with, interestingly enough, the United States Marine Corps. The Mansion hole could not be easily fixed because the large pane of glass would be extremely difficult to remove — they would have to first remove the entire roof to lift the glass out of the building. It was deemed simpler, and perhaps more effective, just to create a spider on the window on the spot of the hole.

21. <u>What was the sentimental reason behind installing an antiques store (The One-of-a-Kind Shop) in New Orleans Square?</u> C. Walt's wife Lillian collected antiques. The merchandise location could never quite match the sales of Disney-specific ones, but it was retained because it added atmosphere and an aura of authenticity to the land. People simply enjoyed browsing through the offerings, which felt like a bit of a relief from the Disneyland outside the shop walls. In 1996, the shop was finally removed in a shuffle of New Orleans shops, which saw the addition of a Christmas themed shop to the area.

22. <u>What part of New Orleans Square was conceived of, and partly built, long before it was finished and opened?</u> A. Haunted Mansion. Originally, this would have been part of Frontierland and was viewed as an extension of a wax museum idea for the western section of Frontierland. Imagineers debated whether the exterior should be musty and scary, but Walt insisted that the outside be pristine while the inside was filled with dust and cobwebs. The house structure was built, without the stretching elevators or show building beyond, in the early 1960s, to be used for a walk-through attraction. When Imagineers returned to the project after their work for the 1964-65 New York

World's Fair, they came armed with a new understanding for the necessity of moving higher quantities of people quickly and the Omnimover system proved capable of doing so. The house sat empty for six years, finally opening in 1969.

23. **Whose face is on the broken statue in the graveyard scene of the Haunted Mansion?** C. Thurl Ravenscroft. Contrary to popular belief (dare we say "urban legend?") this is not Walt Disney, but Thurl, voice of Fritz in the Enchanted Tiki Room, Buff the Buffalo in the Country Bear Playhouse, several voiceovers in Pirates of the Caribbean, the onetime spiel on the Disneyland Railroad steam trains, and best known as the voice of Tony the Tiger in the television commercials. The other four faces are not those of the popular singing group Thurl was in at the time, the Mellomen, as many fans believe (there are only four Mellomen including Thurl, but five busts). The other four faces are Verne Rowe, Jay Meyer, Bob Ebright, and Chuck Schroeder. The Mellomen are, however, well represented at Disneyland; they sing the song "Grim Grinning Ghosts" in the attraction, as well as "Yo Ho (A Pirate's Life for Me)" in Pirates of the Caribbean. They were also prolific in Disney films, having sung "Painting the Roses Red" in *Alice in Wonderland*, "He's a Tramp" as background dogs in *Lady and the Tramp*, and other such 1950s hits as "The Ballad of Davy Crockett." The Mellomen, also onetime backup singers for Elvis Presley, consisted in the 1960s of Thurl Ravenscroft, Max Smith, Bill Cole, and Bill Lee.

24. **Who wrote the lyrics for "Yo Ho (A Pirate's Life for Me)" for Pirates of the Caribbean?** B. X. Atencio. The lyrics include some questionable activities that mirror the action seen in the ride: "Yo ho, yo ho, a pirate's life for me / We pillage, plunder, we rifle and loot / Drink up me 'earties, yo ho / We kidnap and ravage and don't give a hoot / Drink up me 'earties, yo ho." Most Guests leave having only understood "Yo ho, yo ho, a pirate's life for me," however.

25. **Who wrote the music for "Yo Ho (A Pirate's Life for Me)"?** A. George Bruns. George is also the composer responsible for the

theme song to "Davy Crockett." The lyrics were written by X. Atencio, who also wrote the attraction's script and the words to "Grim Grinning Ghosts," the Haunted Mansion's most famous song. Buddy Baker wrote the music for that song.

26. <u>Who penned the lyrics to "Grim Grinning Ghosts"?</u> B. X. Atencio, who had written the show for Adventure Thru Inner Space and created the dialogue for the animated figures in Pirates of the Caribbean, as well as writing the lyrics to the pirates' theme song "Yo Ho (A Pirate's Life for Me)."

Section Three - Difficult

27. <u>What are the various ways Haunted Mansion ghosts are generated?</u> No, not a single one is a hologram. A variety of techniques are used to trick the Guest visually or to insinuate an ethereal presence. Most of the ghosts in the attic and graveyard are standard Audio-Animatronics painted fluorescent and illuminated; film projections are used for Madame Leota (by virtue of a fiber bundle inside her head, projecting the image outward onto the glass), and similar projection tricks are used for the piano ghost in the attic and Little Leota. A one-way mirror is used in conjunction with Audio-Animatronics and lighting on the other side of the mirror to create the wonderful Hitchhiker illusions. This effect is replicated in the Fantasyland Mad Hatter shop, where the Cheshire Cat appears, grins, and fades away right before your eyes; and the effect is also used in Mickey's Barn, where a Sorcerer Mickey appears and disappears in a mirror on the floor. The best ghosts are doubtless in the ballroom, and these are created through an old technique called "Pepper's Ghost": robots are going through the motions you witness, but lighting thrown on them gets reflected in the plate glass between you and the ballroom, making it seem that the images inhabit the empty set you see. Remove the glass, and the

set would look empty! Yale Gracey adapted this effect for the Mansion.

28. **What is the history of the hearse in front of the Haunted Mansion?** The hearse, added in 1996, was supposedly used to carry Mormon leader Brigham Young to his grave, though Young scholars dispute that he had even used a hearse at all. Disneyland bought the hearse from a Malibu collector not so much for its history as for its authenticity and appearance — how many 19th century hearses are preserved in their original condition? — and then shipped it to Anaheim, where it was meticulously renovated and repainted.

29. **How much did New Orleans Square cost to build?** $17 million, the same amount it had cost Walt, eleven years prior, to build all of Disneyland! The high costs were only partly due to inflation; the Pirates of the Caribbean was a highly expensive ride to research and create, in no small part due to its numerous special effects and army of expensive Audio-Animatronics.

30. **Which 1985 theatrical movie had been inspired, particularly in its set design, directly from the Pirates of the Caribbean?** *Goonies.* Steven Spielberg has acknowledged that the cave sequences and design were inspired by the first two sets in Pirates of the Caribbean, especially the colorful echoing waterfalls and twisted rockwork that accompanies the beach scene. One other coup in set design in the attraction is the legacy of the 1964 World's Fair, where Disney introduced four other attractions: the moving clouds in the town sequences was an effect pioneered by Disney for the G.E. Skydome Spectacular (which showed mankind harnessing fire). Large 10" by 10" projectors are used to create the effect of a sky in motion, seen in the Pirates attraction as realistic clouds.

31. **Who provided the voice for the Ghost Host?** Paul Frees. At Disneyland, Frees has been the narrator for Adventure Thru Inner Space and Great Moments with Mr. Lincoln. He also voiced Ludwig Von Drake on the Disneyland TV show.

32. **How did the Trophy Room in Club 33 get its name?** This room, separate from the main dining room, was conceived as a kind of rich man's hunting lodge, with stuffed animal heads along the walls.

33. **Who designed the costumes for the pirates in the Pirates of the Caribbean?** Alice Davis, lead designer Marc Davis' wife. Though she was told not to incur the expense, she had a second set of costumes prepared before the ride even opened, as a precaution. It became necessary after a real fire in the Burning City stage to use her second set of costumes — thus, due to her foresight, the ride never had a delay resulting from the costumes lost in the fire!

Critter Country

Critter Country
Questions

1. What Disney movie is Splash Mountain based on?
   a. *So Dear to My Heart*
   b. *Fun and Fancy Free*
   c. *Song of the South*
   d. *Make Mine Music*

2. What is the first song sung by the Audio-Animatronics on Splash Mountain?
   a. "Zip-A-Dee-Doo-Dah"
   b. "Ev'rybody Has a Laughing Place"
   c. "Burrows Lament"
   d. "How Do You Do"

3. What does Brer Bear find when he goes looking for Brer Rabbit's Laughing Place?
   a. Bees
   b. Wasps
   c. Tar
   d. Scorpions

4. What is the name of the theater where the bears sang?
   a. Country Bear Theater
   b. Country Bear Amphitheater
   c. Country Bear Cave
   d. Country Bear Playhouse

5. What animals hang from the ceiling in Splash Mountain?
   a. Baby weasels
   b. Baby turtles
   c. Baby opossums
   d. Baby rabbits

6. What kind of Boy Scout was the Baby Bear Oscar in the Country Bear Playhouse?
   a. Cub Scout
   b. Eagle Scout
   c. Tiger Cub Scout
   d. Varsity Scout

7. Which was not one of the three Country Bear shows?
   a. Country Bear Jamboree
   b. Country Bear Hoedown
   c. Country Bear Vacation Hoedown
   d. Country Bear Christmas Special

8. What was the name of the female bear swinging from the ceiling?
  a. Teddi Barra
  b. Bunny
  c. Trixie
  d. Bubbles

Section Two - Medium

9. In what year did Bear Country open?
  a. 1968
  b. 1969
  c. 1970
  d. 1971
  e. 1972
  f. 1973

10. Where did Imagineer Tony Baxter think up the idea for Splash Mountain?
  a. In his office
  b. In his car on the freeway
  c. While sitting in Bear Country
  d. While riding the Matterhorn Bobsleds
  e. While watching *Song of the South*
  f. While walking down Main Street

11. Which of the Five Bear Rugs played the banjo?
    a. Tennessee
    b. Fred
    c. Zeb
    d. Ted
    e. Zeke
    f. Oscar

12. What were the names of the three stuffed heads in the Country Bear Playhouse?
    a. Max, Mike, Melvin
    b. Max, Mike, Buff
    c. Max, Buff, Melvin
    d. Mike, Buff, Mitch
    e. Mike, Buff, Melvin
    f. Mitch, Buff, Melvin

13. According to the sign next to it, what is the name of the first drop on Splash Mountain?
    a. Critter Falls
    b. Briar Patch Falls
    c. Chickapin Falls
    d. Slippin' Falls
    e. Br'er Falls
    f. Splash Falls

14. What was the Brer Bar called before Splash Mountain?
    a. Mile Long Bar
    b. Critter Bar

c. Bear Bar

d. Pretzel Bar

e. Bear Outpost

f. Bear Breaks

15. What was the name of the bear dressed up as Elvis and singing "We Can Make It to the Top"?

    a. Terrence the Shaker

    b. Henry

    c. Wendell

    d. Ernest "The Dude"

    e. Liver Lips McGrowl

    f. Big Al

16. When Bear Country opened, there was already a "Bear Country" along the tracks of Mine Train Through Nature's Wonderland. How many years did both Bear Countries coexist?

    a. One

    b. Two

    c. Three

    d. Four

    e. Five

    f. Six

17. What structures were added throughout the land to reinforce its new theme when the land changed from Bear Country to Critter Country?

18. What song was changed in the Splash Mountain show prior to its opening in 1989?

19. What was Splash Mountain's claim to fame in 1989?

20. What is the wooden peak at the top of Splash Mountain called?

21. Who lent his vocal talent for recording the lines for Brer Bear in Splash Mountain?

22. Who was the ranger of Bear Country, as listed on the welcome sign?

23. On what date did The Many Adventures of Winnie the Pooh officially open?

Critter Country
Answers

Section One - Easy

1. <u>**What Disney movie is Splash Mountain based on?**</u> C. *Song of the South*. This 1946 movie was part live-action and part animated. Its genteel depiction of life in the post-slavery South came under fire for racism, but Disney had consulted with black leaders before the picture was made precisely to avoid such problems. Any lingering notion of racism is completely absent in the ride, however. The Tar Baby sequence from the movie, for example, has been replaced with Brer Rabbit stuck in honey.

2. <u>**What is the first song sung by the Audio-Animatronics on Splash Mountain?**</u> D. "How Do You Do." This song comes from the movie *Song of the South* just like the other, more recognizable songs "Zip-A-Dee-Doo-Dah" and "Ev'rybody Has a Laughing Place." The first song occurs as Guests finally enter the mountain itself rather than traversing around it. Like Space Mountain, Splash Mountain was sunk into the ground when built so as to avoid overshadowing Disneyland's existing icons, the Matterhorn and Sleeping Beauty Castle.

3. <u>**What does Brer Bear find when he goes looking for Brer Rabbit's Laughing Place?**</u> A. Bees. As we round the corner, we see Brer Rabbit laughing and Brer Bear's large behind; he says rather loudly "There's nothing in here but...BEES!" and the last word is timed to correspond with our log's sudden plunge into a waterless drop, followed by an immediate upramp back into water. This so-called "dip-drop" can occur because the logs also

have wheels that help the log work, for a brief moment, like a rollercoaster car on a track.

4. <u>What was the name of the theater where the bears sing?</u> D. Country Bear Playhouse. The Playhouse was actually two theaters, not just one. Each held 306 seats on padded benches. If you looked closely you could spot two styles intertwining in the theater's design: Victorian and "backwoods rustic." The hillbilly element was obvious in the talking stuffed heads and the natural wood paneling, while the Victorian decor could be seen in the gold proscenium at the top of the stage, which informed us that Ursus H. Bear, the Founder, lived from 1848-1928. The idea was that the combination of styles lent the entire structure a homey, family-friendly tone that was both familiar and exotic. The theaters covered 5,400 square feet and had a combined capacity of over 1,800 guests per hour.

5. <u>What animals hang from the ceiling in Splash Mountain?</u> C. Baby opossums. They are visible among the ceiling foliage just before Drop #2, which is really just a few feet tall. An argument could also be made for the weasel, who pops out of holes in the floor and ceiling of the Laughin' Place much as he did from barrels and crates in America Sings.

6. <u>What kind of Boy Scout was the Baby Bear Oscar in the Country Bear Playhouse?</u> A. Cub Scout. A young visitor to the show, himself a Cub Scout, noticed that the bear was wearing the wrong colored handkerchief for a Cub Scout, and he wrote to Disneyland about it, even offering his own handkerchief to correct the mistake. Pleased by the response, Disneyland thanked the boy and fixed the show with his donation, and communicated the entire inspiring story to the Cast Members through the employee newsletter.

7. <u>Which was not one of the three Country Bear shows?</u> B. Country Bear Hoedown. The real shows were: The Country Bear Jamboree, which first debuted at Walt Disney World Resort and ran at Disneyland from 1971-1986; The Country

Bear Christmas Special, which debuted in 1984 and ran during the holiday season; and The Country Bear Vacation Hoedown, the new show which, in 1986, displaced the original show from Disneyland. Confusingly, the Japanese named their show "The Country Bear Vacation Jamboree," an amalgamation of two titles of the American shows, and a poster from their show hung in the Anaheim theater! Although the Japanese title combines the names from two shows, their presentation is a version of the Vacation Hoedown. The Country Bear Playhouse closed permanently at Disneyland in September 2001.

8. **What was the name of the female bear swinging from the ceiling?** A. Teddi Barra. She sang "Singing (and Swinging) in the Rain" in the Vacation show. In the holiday show, she sang "Chestnuts Roasting on an Open Fire."

Section Two - Medium

9. **In what year did Bear Country open?** E. 1972. The idea was to create a new corner of the Park that would lure more people away from the crowded zones of Fantasyland and Tomorrowland and into the wide areas of Frontierland and Bear Country. To that end, the narrow walkways into the Indian village (initially conceived in 1956 as tunnels, but never built that way) were replaced with a broad avenue, but all this space only highlighted the emptiness once Guests became used to the Country Bear Jamboree, really the only attraction in Bear Country. The Park distribution would only become more equalized with the addition of Splash Mountain in 1989.

10. **Where did Imagineer Tony Baxter think up the idea for Splash Mountain?** B. In his car on the freeway. He had been considering Bear Country, a relatively unpopulated portion of the Park, and Disneyland's need of a new thrill ride. He had already considered using the Audio-Animatronics from America

Sings, another low-attended attraction, and suddenly realized while stuck in traffic on Interstate 5 that the existing robots could be used in a flume attraction, and he hit upon *Song of the South* as the inspiration for the Disney theme to the ride. Some elements of the ride owe their existence to the "Western River Expedition," a never-built extravaganza on the scale of Pirates of the Caribbean. The Expedition was to have been narrated at frequent points by an owl named Hoots Gibson, and an homage to Hoots can be seen in the owl near the waterfall upramp at the start of the ride (and later, hawking in-ride photos at the attraction's conclusion).

11. **Which of the Five Bear Rugs played the banjo?** E. Zeke. Other Bear Rugs and their instruments: Zeb (Fiddle); Ted (Cornjug); Fred (Mouth Harp); Tennessee (the one-string "thing"). Zeb's son Oscar just sat and listened to the music.

12. **What were the names of the three stuffed heads in the Country Bear Playhouse?** C. Max, Buff, Melvin. The deer was named Max, the buffalo was called Buff, and Melvin was the stuffed moose. Melvin played the stupid one that the others good-naturedly made fun of.

13. **According to the sign next to it, what is the name of the first drop on Splash Mountain?** D. Slippin' Falls. The name is an obvious play on the term "slip and fall," and this drop and straightaway shoot your log into the show building outside the berm. Most Guests are too busy thrilling at the drop, avoiding getting wet (or trying to get wet!) to notice that they're entering that building, which is pretty well themed anyway.

14. **What was the Brer Bar called before Splash Mountain?** A. Mile Long Bar. Its name was derived from the mirrors facing each other on either end of the bar, so that looking into one mirror meant actually seeing an infinite regress of mirrors: the bar looked like it was a mile long. In 2003, this facility became part of Pooh Corner when The Many Adventures of Winnie the Pooh opened next door.

15. <u>What was the name of the bear dressed up as Elvis and singing "We Can Make It to the Top"?</u> E. Liver Lips McGrowl. Meanwhile, the overweight bear, Trixie, lamented lost love; the Sun Bonnets (Bunny, Bubbles and Beulah) sang happy songs; Wendell shot either a camera or a shotgun at the audience; Ernest played violin and avoided bees; Terrence the Shaker tried to make inter-species relationships work; and Gomer pounded on the piano. Our host Henry re-appeared occasionally to introduce the performers, though he only sang at the finale.

16. <u>When Bear Country opened, there was already a "Bear Country" along the tracks of Mine Train Through Nature's Wonderland. How many years did both Bear Countries coexist?</u> E. Five. Both Bear Countires existed from 1972 until 1977, when Nature's Wonderland was razed to prepare the way for Big Thunder Mountain Railroad.

Section Three - Difficult

17. <u>What structures were added throughout the land to reinforce its new theme when the land changed from Bear Country to Critter Country?</u> Small wooden houses were added to the babbling brook that runs the length of most of the land, as if to imply that the entire area is populated by little "critters" that always somehow manage to remain out of sight.

18. <u>What song was changed in the Splash Mountain show prior to its opening in 1989?</u> Originally, the mother rabbit (between the Laughing Place and the upramp) sang "Burrows Lament" (a.k.a. "Sooner or Later"), a tune still heard in Critter Country as orchestral area music. The refrain for the song was "sooner or later that rabbit is gonna come hooooooome, he's learned his lesson again." The tune was melancholic, rather than menacing, so several months after opening the switch was made to the

current song. The mother rabbit now sings "Stay away from the Laughing Place / You must beware the fox is there! / Don't go in! / That Brer Fox has got his way / The Laughing Place this very day / What can poor Brer Rabbit do / To keep from becoming rabbit stew?"

19. **What was Splash Mountain's claim to fame in 1989?** It was the world's tallest drop on a water flume, at fifty-two-and-a-half feet, and also the world's steepest, at 47 degrees. The record has since been broken, but the drop on Splash Mountain remains terrifying for many Guests, though the fact that the last several feet are not visible from the queue line make it look less tall from the outside than it would otherwise.

20. **What is the wooden peak at the top of Splash Mountain called?** Chickapin Hill. This name comes from the film *Song of the South*, where it was the hideout of Brer Fox and Brer Bear. The hollowed-out log hid a small cave beneath it, which roughly corresponds to the layout at Disneyland; Brer Rabbit is held captive just below the peak, and the drop is symbolic of his being thrown into the briar patch below.

21. **Who lent his vocal talent for recording the lines for Brer Bear in Splash Mountain?** Nick Stewart. This 70-year-old actor had supplied the bear's voice in 1946 for the original movie as well. That's not the first time a voice actor has been recalled for Disneyland, however. Adriana Caselotti's voice is used at the Snow White Wishing Well. For the Fantasyland rehab, Kathryn Beaumont, the voice of Alice, returned thirty years after the film to reprise her role.

22. **Who was the ranger of Bear Country, as listed on the welcome sign?** J. Audubon Woodlore. The sign read: "A honey of a place since '72. Permits must be obtained for tree-climbing, fishing, scratching and hibernating (permanent residents excepted). No permit necessary for feeding bears. — J. Audubon Woodlore, Park Ranger."

23. **On what date did The Many Adventures of Winnie the Pooh officially open?** April 11, 2003. Built on the land which housed the Country Bear Playhouse, the Pooh attraction features vehicles that are individually named, continuing a tradition present on most Disney dark rides. The Pooh vehicles are named after characters like Pooh, Tigger, Kanga, Roo, or Rabbit, as well as theme words like Floody, Blustery, Bouncy, or Hunny. Though there were only 22 vehicles, 24 names were created, as two extra bumpers were made and the vehicle names were carved into the bumpers.

Miscellaneous

Miscellaneous Questions

Section One - Easy

1. Which land in Disneyland is the largest in terms of area?
   - a. Tomorrowland
   - b. Fantasyland
   - c. Critter Country
   - d. Frontierland

2. What was the name of the fireworks show when it debuted in 1956?
   - a. Believe in the Magic
   - b. Fun in the Sky
   - c. Fantasy in the Sky
   - d. Tinker Bell's Treat

3. Which Disneyland watercraft is/are not on rails or in a flume?
   - a. Rafts to Tom Sawyer Island
   - b. Sailing Ship Columbia
   - c. Mark Twain Riverboat
   - d. Pirates of the Caribbean

4. Disneyland has had three systems for ride payment. Which was <u>not</u> one of them?
    a. Pay by coins
    b. Debit card system
    c. "A" through "E" tickets
    d. Unlimited use passport

5. What is the oldest object in Disneyland?
    a. Gas lamps on Main Street
    b. Cannon on Main Street
    c. Petrified tree in Frontierland
    d. Eucalyptus trees between Main Street and Adventureland

6. Where in Disneyland can you find a picture of Roy O. Disney?
    a. City Hall
    b. Opera House
    c. John Colter Building
    d. Fowler's Inn

7. Which of the following does <u>not</u> have a population sign?
    a. Frontierland Train Station
    b. Main Street Train Station
    c. Mickey's Toontown gate
    d. Big Thunder Mountain Railroad

8. How many lands does Disneyland now have?
    a. Six
    b. Seven

c. Eight

d. Nine

9. Where in Disneyland are the animals
   stuffed rather than mechanized?
   a. "it's a small world"
   b. Big Thunder Mountain Railroad
   c. Pirates of the Caribbean
   d. Grand Canyon Diorama

10. What was the name of the Disney-owned
    RV campground near Disneyland?
    a. Disney's RV Party
    b. Disney's Fort Wilderness
    c. Disney's Davy Crockett
       Campgrounds
    d. Disney's Vacationland
       Campground

11. What two types of trees were grown on
    the Disneyland site before it was
    purchased for development?
    a. Oranges and walnuts
    b. Oranges and cypress
    c. Oranges and lemons
    d. Lemons and cypress

12. Where can you find the Disney family
    crest?
    a. Country Bear Playhouse
    b. Pinocchio's Daring Journey

c. Innoventions

d. Sleeping Beauty Castle

13. How much did it cost to build Disneyland in 1955?

    a. $7 million

    b. $17 million

    c. $27 million

    d. $37 million

14. Until 1985, Disneyland was scheduled closed during non-peak times on which two days of the week?

    a. Sunday and Monday

    b. Monday and Tuesday

    c. Tuesday and Wednesday

    d. Wednesday and Thursday

15. How many treehouses are there at Disneyland?

    a. One

    b. Two

    c. Three

    d. Four

16. Where are the two first-aid stations located?

    a. End of Main Street and behind Hungry Bear Restaurant

    b. End of Main Street and behind Brer Bar

    c. Town Square and end of Main Street

    d. Town Square and behind "it's a small world"

Section Two - Medium

17. Which was the last E-Ticket ride added to Disneyland before the Park switched to a "Passport system"?

    a. Space Mountain
    b. Submarine Voyage
    c. Big Thunder Mountain Railroad
    d. Captain EO
    e. Splash Mountain
    f. Star Tours

18. Where could we find Saddle-Sore Swanson?

    a. America Sings
    b. Submarine Voyage
    c. Pack Mules
    d. Conestoga Wagon
    e. Mine Train Through Nature's Wonderland
    f. Rainbow Caverns Mine Train

19. Where is the Disneyland time capsule?

    a. Next to Innoventions
    b. Next to Country Bear Playhouse

c. Underneath the Main Street
    Train Station
d. In Mickey's Toontown
e. Inside Sleeping Beauty Castle
f. In front of Sleeping Beauty
    Castle

20. What was the first 3D movie to play at
Disneyland?
    a. *Creature from the Black Lagoon*
    b. *3D Jamboree*
    c. *Captain EO*
    d. *Honey, I Shrunk the Audience*
    e. *Magic Journeys*
    f. *O, Canada*

21. Which A-list comedian used to work at
Disneyland?
    a. Eddie Murphy
    b. Robin Williams
    c. Jerry Seinfeld
    d. Adam Sandler
    e. Jim Carrey
    f. Steve Martin

22. How many cemeteries are there in
Disneyland?
    a. One
    b. Three
    c. Four
    d. Five

e. Seven

f. Eight

23. Where in Disneyland could one find
drawings by Norman Rockwell?
   a. City Hall
   b. Walt Disney Story
   c. Emporium
   d. Mickey's House
   e. Minnie's House
   f. Frontierland shops

24. What Christmas tradition at Disneyland is
more than forty years old?
   a. Candlelight Procession
   b. "it's a small world holiday"
   c. Cookie decorating
   d. Face painting
   e. Country Bear Christmas Special
   f. Tamales sold from vending carts

25. Where was the Toy Story Funhouse
located in 1996?
   a. Videopolis
   b. Small World Way
   c. Big Thunder Ranch
   d. Golden Horseshoe Revue
   e. Critter Country
   f. Space Mountain Concourse

26. In terms of elevation, what was the highest Guest-accessible location at Disneyland in 1956?
    a. Moonliner
    b. Matterhorn Bobsleds
    c. Tom & Huck's Treehouse
    d. Swiss Family Robinson Treehouse
    e. Chip & Dale's Treehouse
    f. Sleeping Beauty Castle Walk-Thru

27. Who was the first Disneyland Ambassador?
    a. Sasha Sherbin
    b. Emily Zinser
    c. Kathleen Mitts
    d. Jennifer Simis
    e. Connie Swanson
    f. Julie Reihm

28. What is the name of the Disneyland Administration building that opened in 1994?
    a. Team Disney Anaheim
    b. Team Disneyland
    c. Global Van Lines
    d. Global Disney Anaheim
    e. Administration
    f. Costuming

29. Where are the monorails stored overnight?
    a. At the Tomorrowland Station
    b. At the Downtown Disney Station
    c. Along the track at Harbor Blvd.
    d. Above the Disneyland Railroad trains backstage
    e. Behind Innoventions
    f. Next to the Matterhorn

30. What foreign leader was denied admission to Disneyland in 1959?
    a. Fidel Castro
    b. Shah of Iran
    c. Nikita Khrushchev
    d. Baby Doc Duvalier
    e. Eva Peron
    f. Che Guevara

31. Which were the first restrooms at Disneyland to have the automated infrared toilets and faucets?
    a. At Space Mountain
    b. At entrance to Adventureland
    c. Near the Tomorrowland Skyway Station
    d. Videopolis
    e. At Bank of America on Main Street
    f. In New Orleans Square

32. Which of the following did <u>not</u> sponsor one of the four attractions Disney created for the 1964 New York's World Fair?
    a. Ford Motor Company
    b. General Motors
    c. General Electric
    d. State of Illinois
    e. UNICEF

Section Three - Difficult

33. What do Imagineers mean when they refer to an "Envelope of Protection"?

34. What were the names of the parking lot sections in the 100-acre parking lot that closed in January 1998?

35. What are the existing attractions in Disneyland to have a song created for them by the Sherman Brothers?

36. Where were the Disneyland Ferris wheels?

37. Are there tunnels connecting all of Disneyland underground?

38. Where was the last original orange tree on the Disney property?

39. What was "Project Little Man"?

40. What is Club 55?

41. Who is acknowledged as the "Voice of Disneyland"?

42. What was the first day Disneyland was scheduled to open, but never did?

43. Who was Disneyland's first entertainment director?

44. What problems developed with the Mickey Mouse Club Circus in Fantasyland during its first season?

45. Which two attractions made use of equipment that so far exceeded the manufacturer's expectations that they sent out engineers to determine why the equipment lasted so long?

46. What two cities competed for Disney's second Southern California theme park?

47. What became of the plans for the ocean-themed park in Southern California?

48. What were the initial plans for the Disneyland Resort expansion in the early 1990s?

49. After the initial summer, what was the first Disneyland ride to miss its scheduled grand opening?

50. When did Disney Dollars debut?

51. In what year was a baby born at Disneyland for the first time?

52. What was the name of the plan Michael Eisner unveiled at Disneyland's 35th Birthday in 1990?

53. What is the name of the branch of Walt Disney Imagineering based at Disneyland?

54. What were the words to Walt's dedication speech of Disneyland at opening in 1955?

Miscellaneous Answers

Section One - Easy

1. <u>Which land in Disneyland is the largest in terms of area?</u> D. Frontierland. In the early days this was even more obviously the case, for it extended into what is now New Orleans Square (Bear/Critter Country was as yet undeveloped). Even with the additions of the new west-side lands, however, Frontierland remains vast, covering the Rivers of America, the island it encircles, the western street, and the Big Thunder area.

2. <u>What was the name of the fireworks show when it debuted in 1956?</u> C. Fantasy in the Sky. It was created by Tommy Walker, who also instituted many other traditions at Disneyland such as Grad Nite and the Dapper Dans barbershop quartet. The fireworks show became "Believe...There's Magic in the Stars" for the 45th Anniversary celebration in 2000, then "Disney's Imagine... A Fantasy in the Sky" in 2004, and "Remember Dreams Come True" in 2005.

3. <u>Which Disneyland watercraft is/are not on rails or in a flume?</u> A. Rafts to Tom Sawyer Island. Another attraction currently operating on the Rivers of America that are free-floating are the Davy Crockett Explorer Canoes; the Mike Fink Keelboats, which once traveled the rivers, also did not run on a track.

4. <u>Disneyland has had three systems for ride payment. Which was not one of them?</u> B. Debit cards. The current system of a "passport" entitling the visitor to unlimited use of all attractions (except the arcades) replaced the popular "ticket system" for good in 1982, though there was a one-year period of overlap

when both systems were in effect. The ticket system was a way to generate interest in the smaller, less visible rides, since tickets for them came bundled in the ticket books. A system from A-C, then A-D, and finally A-E was developed, and an E-Ticket came to represent the best Disneyland had to offer. When astronaut Sally Ride called the Space Shuttle a "real E-Ticket ride," it was clear to all that she meant a ride with great thrills and rewards. The ticket system replaced a coin-collection system; in the beginning, visitors would have to pay — with cash — each time they wanted admission to a particular attraction. The ticket books, once introduced, also reduced the Guests' impression that they were constantly going to their wallet all day long.

5.   <u>What is the oldest object in Disneyland?</u> C. The petrified tree located along the shores of the Rivers of America, just south of the Mark Twain Riverboat loading dock, is by far the oldest thing in Disneyland. Its plaque reads: "Petrified Tree — From the Pike Petrified Forest, Colorado — This section weighs five tons and measures 7½ feet in diameter. The original tree, estimated to have been 200 feet tall, was part of a sub-tropical forest 55 to 70 million years ago in what is now Colorado. Scientists believe it to be of the redwood of Sequoia species. During some prehistoric era a cataclysmic upheaval caused silica laden water to overspread the living forest. Wood cells were changed during the course of time to sandstone. Opals were formed within the tree trunk itself."

6.   <u>Where in Disneyland can you find a picture of Roy O. Disney?</u> B. Opera House. His portrait is at the entrance to the Walt Disney Story. These portraits of Roy and Walt are among the very few to be found in the Park (there is another one is in the Mark Twain Wheelhouse). Roy very rarely posed for pictures; he preferred to stay out of the spotlight.

7.   <u>Which of the following does not have a population sign?</u> A. Frontierland Train Station. One does exist at the train depot on Main Street (at this printing, 450 million); at Toontown, where a whimsical sign constantly changes the number and even

inserts nonsense symbols; and at the Big Thunder Mountain Railroad (38).

8. **How many lands does Disneyland now have?** C. Eight. Main Street, U.S.A. (1955), Tomorrowland (1955), Fantasyland (1955), Mickey's Toontown (1993), Adventureland (1955), Frontierland (1955), New Orleans Square (1966), and Critter Country (opened as Bear Country in 1972, name changed in 1988).

9. **Where in Disneyland are the animals stuffed rather than mechanized?** D. Grand Canyon Diorama. Here, the animals are real taxidermic animals. Guests were spared any noxious odors when the diorama opened, however, because glass separated the exhibit from the passing trains.

10. **What was the name of the Disney-owned RV campground near Disneyland?** D. Disney's Vacationland Campground. This property, which opened in 1971 and closed in 1997 to prepare for the Resort expansion, was located along West Street, on the current site of the large "Mickey & Friends" Disneyland parking structure.

11. **What two types of trees were grown on the Disneyland site before it was purchased for development?** A. Oranges and walnuts. The trees were organized into groves, with more than 12,000 trees altogether. The land had come from a Spanish land grant, the Rancho San Juan Cajon de Santa Ana grant.

12. **Where can you find the Disney family crest?** D. Sleeping Beauty Castle. The crest is located on the front face of the castle, right above the arch that leads through it. Just inside the castle is the Castle Heraldry Shoppe, where family crests from around the world can be viewed and purchased with a family history, put on a parchment suitable for framing. Most names can be found; yes, even Disney.

13. **How much did it cost to build Disneyland in 1955?** B. $17 million. Much of this money was raised by deals with ABC,

Bank of America, and Western Printing and Lithographing, who partly owned Disneyland as a result. ABC contributed $500,000 and promised $4.5 million in loans, in return for a 34.48% ownership of the Park. In 1960, Disney bought out the ABC investment in Disneyland for $7.5 million. Much later, in 1995, Disney bought all of ABC/Capital Cities itself. They have yet to buy Bank of America, however!

14. **Until 1985, Disneyland was scheduled closed during non-peak times on which two days of the week?** B. Monday and Tuesday. Until February 6, 1985, Disneyland was scheduled to be closed on Mondays and Tuesdays during the off-season. No one really thought that an amusement park could make money year-round by staying open every day of the week; most were open only on holiday periods and sometimes on weekends. Disneyland changed all that by providing a reason for people to create "work vacations."

15. **How many treehouses are there at Disneyland?** D. Four. Chip 'n Dale's Treehouse, Tarzan's Treehouse, and Tom and Huck's Treehouse on Tom Sawyer Island are the only ones available to Guests to walk through, but there is a "Treehouse of Technology" on display at Innoventions in Tomorrowland.

16. **Where are the two first-aid stations located?** B. End of Main Street and behind Brer Bar. Central First Aid, which is always open and staffed with a registered nurse and/or a doctor, is at the north end of Main Street. On busy days, there was formerly a secondary station opened and staffed; it was located behind the Brer Bar in Critter Country. This way, wheelchairs, nurses, or medical supplies could more quickly reach the western extremities of the Park on days when Disneyland was crowded.

Section Two - Medium

17. <u>Which was the last E-Ticket ride added to Disneyland before the Park switched to a "Passport system"?</u> C. Big Thunder Mountain Railroad. It opened in 1979, two years before the passport system was inaugurated (and three years before the A-E ticket system was discontinued). Splash Mountain opened in 1989, Star Tours in 1987, Captain EO in 1986 (both of them after E-Tickets had been phased out), Space Mountain in 1977 (just before Big Thunder Mountain Railroad), and the Submarine Voyage, which debuted in 1959, was the first E-Ticket ride.

18. <u>Where could we find Saddle-Sore Swanson?</u> A. America Sings. He was a character in America Sings, in the Western segment of the show. Presumably, he was sore from sitting on the saddle of his horse! Here is his complete song: "Well, come along boys and listen to my tale, and I'll tell you all my troubles on the old Chisholm Trail. Come 'a tie yi yippie yippie yay. Come 'a tie yi yippie yippie yay. Now, I went to the boss to draw my roll and he had me figured nine dollars in the hole. Ay, ay, ay, ay."

19. <u>Where is the Disneyland time capsule?</u> F. In front of Sleeping Beauty Castle. In the Castle forecourt, near the giant compass, you can find the location marked as the home of the time capsule. It was created for the 40th anniversary of Disneyland in 1995, and is not to be unearthed and opened until an additional 40 years have transpired; thus, it is set to be opened in 2035. Inside was placed numerous items from 1995, including copies of the current souvenir guides to Disneyland, show schedules, and the Cast Member newsletter.

20. <u>What was the first 3D movie to play at Disneyland?</u> B. *3D Jamboree*. This movie played in the Fantasyland Theatre, which was followed in later years by the Magic Eye Theater in Tomorrowland. The latter was home to *Magic Journeys* and

Captain EO, and the Imagination Institute, where *Honey, I Shrunk the Audience* plays.

21. <u>Which A-list comedian used to work at Disneyland?</u> F. Steve Martin. He worked in Merlin's Magic Shop in Fantasyland. There, his free spirit flourished amid the prankster attitude which characterized the Magic Shop, playing pranks on Guests and fellow workers.

22. <u>How many cemeteries are there in Disneyland?</u> F. Eight. Along the Rivers of America (on the fenced-off part of the island) are the Indian burial grounds, near Fort Wilderness is one for settlers, there is one inside the Frontierland Shooting Gallery, and there are no less than four at the Haunted Mansion: a pet cemetery greets Guests in line, followed by the humorous hillside cemetery, and then there is the graveyard finale within attraction. One more is hidden to all but special-assistance Guests, who enter through the western side of the building and see the original pet cemetery, which inspired the one other Guests can now see in the normal queue. The 8th and final cemetery is outside Alice's cottage in Storybook Land.

23. <u>Where in Disneyland could one find drawings by Norman Rockwell?</u> B. Walt Disney Story. Pencil sketches of Walt's two daughters, Sharon and Diane, hang in Walt's "Formal Office." These are actually copies, as his daughters wanted to hang on to the originals. Rockwell has another connection with Disney; it was his "Saturday Evening Post" magazine covers that served as inspiration for the original miniature scenes done by Ken Anderson when the traveling exhibit "Disneylandia" was first conceived.

24. <u>What Christmas tradition at Disneyland is more than forty years old?</u> A. Candlelight Procession. In the late 1990s Disneyland increasingly began to stress the Christmas season as a special time in the Magic Kingdom and to "claim it" in the way that local parks Knott's Berry Farm and Six Flags Magic Mountain had "claimed" Halloween. To that end, an increasing emphasis

on atmosphere talent and decorating began to appear at Disneyland, and "it's a small world" became "it's a small world holiday" on an annual basis. The Candlelight Procession continued as well, of course, but in the Fantasyland Theater (where it was renamed the "Candlelight Ceremony") instead of the traditional show in Town Square.

25. <u>Where was the Toy Story Funhouse located in 1996?</u> F. Space Mountain Concourse, above the Magic Eye Theater and the Space Place. This temporary attraction reproduced the funhouse which had been located at the El Capitan Theater, where Toy Story had had its premiere. Guests traversed up the ramps (now the normal queue for Space Mountain) and at the top were given "footstands" to tie onto their feet to turn each of them into an honorary "Green Army Man." Then, Guests entered the tent and navigated the pseudo-obstacle course (mostly painted floors and jungle gyms) before exiting out the other side.

26. <u>In terms of elevation, what was the highest Guest-accessible location at Disneyland in 1956?</u> C. Tom & Huck's Tree House. Surprisingly, the highest point then is now just somewhere in the middle in the range. Tom & Huck's Tree House on Tom Sawyer Island won top honors in 1956, before any of the Disneyland Mountain range existed and before Guests were allowed into Sleeping Beauty Castle in 1957.

27. <u>Who was the first Disneyland Ambassador?</u> F. Julie Reihm (Caseletto), in 1965. The others were, in this order: Connie Swanson (Lane) in 1966, Marcia Miner (Phillips) in 1967, Sally Sherbin in 1968, Shari Bescos (Koch) in 1969, Cathy Birk in 1970, Marva Dickson (Thomas) in 1971, Emily Zinser in 1972, Bonnie Drury (Cook) in 1973, Carol DeKeyser (Mezzano) in 1974, Kathy Smith (Hall) in 1975, Christina Schendel (Walker) in 1976, Susan Donald (Edwards) in 1977, Raellen Lescault in 1978, Leona Dombroske (Ross) in 1979, Nancy Englert (Murray) in 1980, Willie Van Der Zwaag (Burckle) in 1981, Joanne Crawford in 1982, Mindy Wilson in 1983, Ellen Coleman (Marchese) in 1984, Melissa Tyler in 1985, Barbara Warren in

1986, Kendra Howell in 1987, Carolyn Long in 1988, Wendy Freeland (Shoeman) in 1989, Jennifer Faust in 1990, Jill Ornelas in 1991, Suzanne Palmiter in 1992, Kathleen Mitts in 1993, Bonnie Delehoy in 1994, Michelle Tryon, Julia Onder, Gerry Aquino in 1995 (the first year with multiple ambassadors), Chris Allen, Gina Purugganan, Heather Thompson, Janet Tanasugarn in 1996, Robyn Schatz, Christina McGeorge, Cathie Milam in 1997, Oscar Carrasco, Dorothy Stratton in 1998, Dorell Mitter, Jennifer Simis (for an eighteen-month tenure) in 1999, Heri "Eddie" Garcia and Doina Roman Osborn (also for an eighteen-month tenure) in 2000, Matt Ebeling in 2002, Daina Baker in 2003, Becky Murphy in 2004, and Andrae Rivas and Rebecca Phelps in 2005.

28. **What is the name of the Disneyland Administration building that opened in 1994?** A. Team Disney Anaheim. The naming scheme was begun in Burbank, the corporate headquarters, which housed the original "Team Disney" building (this is the Michael Graves-designed building, with the dwarfs holding up the roof), and the theme park administrations then began to name their own headquarters in a similar fashion. The green and yellow TDA building sits backstage, along the Interstate 5 freeway, on the site of the former Global Van Lines building.

29. **Where are the monorails stored overnight?** D. Above the Disneyland Railroad trains backstage. This Roundhouse is home not only to the monorails and Disneyland Railroad trains, but also to the service units which clean and inspect the monorail tracks after hours.

30. **What foreign leader was denied admission to Disneyland in 1959?** C. Nikita S. Khrushchev. The then premier of the Soviet Union had wanted to visit, but the U.S. Secret Service determined they could not guarantee his safety, so he threw a temper tantrum by removing his shoe and pounding a table with it. Walt had planned to welcome him by showing him the Submarine Voyage, home of the eighth-largest sub fleet in the world!

31. <u>Which were the first restrooms at Disneyland to have the automated infrared toilets and faucets?</u> D. Videopolis. The system had been installed in 1989 at Walt Disney World Resort but had yet to become mainstream outside of Disney, so for many Guests, the toilets at Videopolis, new in 1990, represented their first exposure to a now-common bathroom "fixture."

32. <u>Which of the following did not sponsor one of the four attractions Disney created for the 1964 New York's World Fair?</u> B. General Motors. The Ford Motor Company sponsored the Magic Skyway, which took riders in Ford cars back through a primeval world and the dawn of mankind; the State of Illinois sponsored the Lincoln exhibit; UNICEF sponsored "it's a small world," and General Electric sponsored Progressland. Each of these attractions came back to Disneyland, and Walt thus accomplished a goal of getting attractions cheaply, paid for by the companies who sponsored them. A secondary goal for him with the New York fair was to establish that Americans on the East Coast enjoyed the Disney product, which helped him to finalize plans for "Project X" — a second Disney theme park in Florida.

Section Three - Difficult

33. <u>What do Imagineers mean when they refer to an "Envelope of Protection"?</u> The term refers to the relationship between riders on a Disneyland attraction and the sets which surround them; they have learned that each ride vehicle must be surrounded by the "envelope" of space which protects the sets from the sometimes destructive riders. This lesson was learned on Adventure Thru Inner Space, where the sets were so close to the riders that they were often destroyed. When the dark rides in Fantasyland were rebuilt in the 1983 rehab, Imagineers kept the "Envelope of Protection" in mind and thus left the sets out of reach of destructive Guests. The idea is not foolproof; the apple

held out by the Queen in Snow White was still stolen so often that it eventually had to be replaced by a hologram-like image in a parabolic mirror.

34. **What were the names of the parking lot sections in the 100-acre parking lot that closed in January 1998?** In the original parking area, the lots were: Alice (the Cast Member parking area), Bambi, Chip, Donald, Eeyore, Flower, Goofy, Happy, Jiminy Cricket, Kanga, King Louie, Mickey, Minnie, Owl, Pinocchio, Robin Hood, Sleepy, Tinker Bell, Thumper, and Winnie the Pooh. One small plot of land in this lot was actually never owned by Disney — the owner refused to sell back in 1955 and Disney leased the land for all those years. After Disney's California Adventure was built, Disney continued to lease the land; the plot in question is in the Paradise Pier section of DCA. In 1998 the original parking lot closed and four new ones were opened: Timon (the last remnant of the original lot), Simba (next to the Disneyland Pacific Hotel), Pinocchio (next to the Disneyland Hotel), and Pumbaa (located on the site of the former Grand Hotel). In the summer of 2000, the "Mickey & Friends" Parking Structure was opened next to the former Pinocchio parking area. In April 2003, the lots for Downtown Disney were renamed Lilo, Stitch, and Zazu (the latter replacing part of Simba). Most Cast Members park at the Katella Cast Member Lot, located (as the name implies) on Katella Avenue. Adjacent to the Katella lot is the Buzz Lightyear lot, an overflow lot built after the parking structure.

35. **What are the existing attractions in Disneyland to have a song created for them by the Sherman Brothers?** "it's a small world," the Enchanted Tiki Room, and Innoventions. Music composed by the two brothers plays in the Main Street Music Loop as well, but this can't be defined as an "attraction." They had also written "Miracles from Molecules," "The Mine Train Song," "Great Big Beautiful Tomorrow," and "Magic Highways of Tomorrow," but the attractions for which these songs were written do not exist at Disneyland today. Richard and Robert Sherman are the songwriting duo responsible for some of the

most memorable music in Disney films, including the songs in *Mary Poppins*, for which they won an Oscar. In 1998 the Sherman Brothers rewrote lyrics to two of their past songs to give a touch of nostalgia to the new Tomorrowland. For Innoventions, "Great Big Beautiful Tomorrow" was rewritten as "Great Big World of Innoventions" (sung by Tom Morrow), and their song "Detroit" from *The Happiest Millionaire* was rewritten as "Magic Highways of Tomorrow" for the Rocket Rods (sung by Nathan Lane, who also voices Tom Morrow).

36. **Where were the Disneyland Ferris wheels?** Long before the Sun Wheel graced Disney's California Adventure, there had been two Ferris wheels inside Disneyland's borders. Both were built by the Eli Bridge Company; one was located at the Central Plaza, and the second was in front of the Main Street Train Station, during the "State Fair" promotions of 1987-1990. The one in the Central Plaza was located where the Gift-Giver Extraordinaire stood during Disneyland's 30th anniversary, and where the Walt and Mickey "Partners" statue can now be found. During 1990, the Dream Machine machine had a platform which raised and lowered with GM car giveaways and remains to this day below the statue of Walt. During the later "State Fairs," a smaller Ferris wheel was also added to Big Thunder Ranch, near the Pigmania show. There was even a small model of a Ferris wheel in Progress City.

37. **Are there tunnels connecting all of Disneyland underground?** Not comprehensively. Rumors to this effect likely surfaced because of the Utilidors, a system of tunnels below the Magic Kingdom in Florida (in fact, their Magic Kingdom is built entirely on the second floor). At Disneyland, only a few lands have underground areas and kitchens, and they are not connected to each other. The biggest are in New Orleans Square, Fantasyland, and Tomorrowland.

38. **Where was the last original orange tree on the Disney property?** At the Oriental Gardens at the Disneyland Hotel. The last tree had been saved from destruction only accidentally, but it was

finally removed in the 1990s. A replacement for that tree stood in its place until the Oriental Gardens section of the Hotel was razed in 1999 to prepare the area for the arrival of Downtown Disney and the expansion of the Disneyland Resort. In the 1950s, they did plan to keep a number of indigenous trees from the original groves, and build around them. To that end, they devised a system to mark the trees to be saved: a green ribbon would mean that tree is to be saved, a red ribbon meant it was to be destroyed. The bulldozer operator, however, was colorblind and razed all the trees he could find! Original orange trees do survive, in a matter of speaking, even in today's Disneyland. Gnarled tree branches seemingly growing out of the water in the "Sunken City" of the Jungle Cruise are actually orange trees turned upside down, with their root system poking out of the water.

39. **What was "Project Little Man"?** Back when Walt was interested in creating Disneylandia, a series of miniature sets with animated figures built to travel around the country, he hired Buddy Ebsen to tap dance so that his movements could be filmed and recorded. The idea was to create a miniaturized tap dancer for one of the small sets. "Little Man" worked perfectly as programmed, and the project gave the Imagineers some valuable experience they would later use to build the full-size Audio-Animatronics of the future.

40. **What is Club 55?** This is not a location, but a more abstract association. There are actually two groups who use the name Club 55. One unofficial use of the name refers to the original sponsors of Disneyland (from 1955), without whom Walt's dream could never have achieved reality. Club 55 also refers to the group of Opening Day Cast Members, the last of which retired from Disneyland on July 31, 1997.

41. **Who is acknowledged as the "Voice of Disneyland"?** Jack Wagner. He provided the recorded spiel outside the Main Gate, the safety spiels ("remain seated please") at "it's a small world" and the Matterhorn Bobsleds, and was for years the voice used

for Park announcements such as the start and end of the day, parade reminders, and other daily announcements. Before Jack, Rex Allen (who also was the voice of the narrator in Carousel of Progress) was the Voice of Disneyland.

42. **What was the first day Disneyland was scheduled to open, but never did?** January 26th, 1956, a day of unusually heavy rain. It's often said that the National Day of Mourning (on November 23, 1963) following the assassination of President Kennedy was the first unscheduled close of Disneyland, yet there were eight other days of unexpected closures (apart from 1/26/56) before the JFK assassination. Disneyland kept its gates closed on December 16, 1987, when a freak storm of hurricane force was predicted for Orange County, and Disneyland preventively decided not to open. Heavy rain led to a further unscheduled closure on December 7, 1992. Finally, Disneyland did not open on September 11, 2001, as the attacks in New York and Washington happened at 6:00 a.m. California time.

43. **Who was Disneyland's first entertainment director?** Tommy Walker, who started many of Disneyland's institutions, including the Candlelight Procession and Fantasy in the Sky. After leaving Disneyland, he went on to orchestrate many of the fireworks displays for significant events and celebrations, and he was the director behind the show at the unveiling of the Statue of Liberty after an extensive renovation — a fireworks extravaganza that was coincidentally used in the finale of *American Journeys* back at Disneyland!

44. **What problems developed with the Mickey Mouse Club Circus in Fantasyland during its first season?** There were numerous problems with the animals: the llamas once escaped and ran down Main Street, tigers and panthers fought, and even the performers, a tough bunch, smoked and cursed like animals themselves. There were also technical glitches: once a section of the tent's roof caved in, and one trapeze artist had her top fall off in mid-flight. The biggest problem was simply attendance; the 2000-seat area was typically less than a quarter full.

45. <u>Which two attractions made use of equipment that so far exceeded the manufacturer's expectations that they sent out engineers to determine why the equipment lasted so long?</u> The actuators at the Flying Saucers and the batteries powering the Mine Train Through Nature's Wonderland (these were not standard locomotives!) both exceeded lifetime expectations. In both cases, the engineers sent out to test the equipment discovered that the daily operating routine and maintenance programs at Disneyland had conspired to produce such clean operating conditions — complete discharge daily and complete recharging nightly — that the equipment would long outlast its rated specifications.

46. <u>What two cities competed for Disney's second Southern California theme park?</u> Anaheim and Long Beach. Because Disney optioned the rights to purchase the Queen Mary and the Spruce Goose, it considered building an ocean-themed Park in Long Beach or a "second gate" adjacent to the original Disneyland in Anaheim. Because it offered more in the way of tax breaks and infrastructure improvements, Anaheim won the bidding war. Additionally, the coastal commission put up roadblocks to the construction of a theme park at the port, further cementing Anaheim as the better choice. Less well known is the "Disney Studios Backlot" proposed park; a theme park planned in 1987 at the Disney Studios' Burbank location. Many of the ideas proposed were later used at the Disney-MGM Studios Park in Walt Disney World Resort.

47. <u>What became of the plans for the ocean-themed park in Southern California?</u> The ideas proposed included a central lagoon and a dramatic volcano, with the Park divided into lands around the volcano. Each would be based in some manner on the ocean and mythologies associated with it. The idea proved too expensive for Long Beach's tastes; elements of the planned Park were incorporated into Tokyo DisneySea, which opened on September 4, 2001.

48. **What were the initial plans for the Disneyland Resort expansion in the early 1990s?** The Disneyland Resort would initially have been the hotels, shopping district, and Disneyland as they exist in their current form, but with "Westcot" as the second theme Park, not Disney's California Adventure. Westcot was to have been a West Coast version of Epcot at Walt Disney World Resort, with exhibits and interactive pavilions, culminating in an astounding 45-minute attraction circling the Park that would have examined the history of the planet, our cultural development, and our role and place in the world. Westcot's price tag was seen as too high by many residents of Anaheim, who would have had to shoulder some of the financial burden, so Disney's California Adventure, a less expensive compromise with an entirely different theme and flavor, was created instead.

49. **After the initial summer, what was the first Disneyland ride to miss its scheduled grand opening?** The Flying Saucers. This popular ride was plagued with mechanical problems and breakdowns during its entire short lifetime at Disneyland, caused mostly by the giant fans under the floor that elevated the saucers. The biggest problem was a harmonic oscillation created by unevenly weighted riders, altering the flow of air upwards throughout the field, so that the force of air was distributed unevenly and finally dissolved itself completely with a loud pop. The uneven oscillation delayed the grand opening of the ride and caused delays and ride breakdowns even after adjustments were made to reduce the problem.

50. **When did Disney Dollars debut?** May 5, 1987. Originally, there were only $1 and $5 denominations, but a $10 bill, designed by Illustrator Matt Mew and featuring Minnie's portrait on the front and a hodgepodge of attractions (Matterhorn Bobsleds, Star Tours, Sleeping Beauty Castle, Splash Mountain) on the reverse, was added in 1989. Minnie was the first female to appear on a bill in America since Martha Washington appeared in the late 1800s on the $1 bills. Disney Dollars were dreamed up by Jack Lindquist, then Vice-President of Marketing at Disneyland (and later Disneyland President). Harry Brice, a

Silhouette Cutter on Main Street, claimed to have submitted the idea to Disneyland's suggestion program for employees, but he failed to prove his case in court.

51. **In what year was a baby born at Disneyland for the first time?** 1979. There have been four babies born at Disneyland, though not intentionally. Disneyland always tries to have the mother brought to a nearby hospital.

52. **What was the name of the plan Michael Eisner unveiled at Disneyland's 35th Birthday in 1990?** "The Disney Decade." Eisner understood that the 1990s would see new Parks added in Florida and Paris, with others under construction in Anaheim and Japan. The film division had come alive and prospered with new animated classics, and merchandising would explode with Disney Stores across the country. New ventures such as cruise lines, sports franchises and television programming, through the acquisition of ABC/Capital Cities, helped bulk up the company.

53. **What is the name of the branch of Walt Disney Imagineering based at Disneyland?** The Disneyland Design Studio. Though their primary responsibility is in making day-to-day artistic decisions about the Park, they are also instrumental in all refurbishments and new construction.

54. **What were the words to Walt's dedication speech of Disneyland at opening in 1955?** "To all who come to this happy place — Welcome. Disneyland is your land. Here, age relives fond memories of the past, and here youth may savor the challenge and promise of the future. Disneyland is dedicated to the ideals, the dreams, and the hard facts that have created America — with the hope that it will be a source of joy and inspiration to all the world." These words are now inscribed on a plaque in Town Square, at the base of the flagpole, and in direct line of sight with Sleeping Beauty Castle.

Postscript

Keeping up with Disneyland history can be endlessly frustrating, tiring, and taxing – but it's also endlessly fascinating, rewarding, and fun. The deeper one looks, it seems, the more the connections between people, projects, and places seem to emerge. The interwoven details and histories combine to form the rich textures that constitute the famed "Disney Magic." To acknowledge the nostalgia, homages, and insider jokes at Disneyland is to experience the totality of immersion in the Disney culture, as if experiencing "Disney Magic" again for the first time.

We hope that readers of "Magic Quizdom" have as much fun reading the book as we had in researching and writing it. Naturally, we hope you learned a thing or two about Disneyland in the process! There's much more to say about Disneyland and its rich and varied history, and we've only just begun. We are hard at work already creating our newest Disneyland publication. Until then, keep Walt's mantra in mind: "Disneyland will never be completed as long as there is imagination left in the world." However Disneyland continues to evolve, one thing is certain: the future will always be anchored in the past, and the richness of its offerings will be seen in its details.

About the Authors

Kevin Yee, a Disney fan from birth, spent the better part of a decade working at Disneyland and cultivating a never-ending fascination with the Park's rich traditions and history. Though his "day job" is in the field of education, his thoughts are never far from Walt's favorite creation in Anaheim.

Jason Schultz, a lifelong fan of the original Disneyland, can distinctly remember the day in 1995 when he became interested in knowing more about the Park's history and the resulting years of research and fun that led to the book before you. No doubt, his hunger for all things Disneyland will not abate.

Their Disney books may be purchased online at http://www.zauberreichpress.com